CAREER
3.0

Celebrating 35 Years of
Penguin Random House India

ADVANCE PRAISE FOR THE BOOK

'Anticipate living to 100, then imagine the need to perpetually evolve your skills to stay pertinent, be it in entrepreneurship or employment. *Career 3.0* is a navigation tool, steering you through the unforeseeable future. Pro-tip: start your journey by delving into the remarkable sketch notes in the book. They're spectacular'—**Peter Shankman, author of *The Boy with the Faster Brain***

'Abhijit's newest work is timed perfectly as many are looking to either reset their careers after the pandemic or experiencing a fast-evolving work environment even in their current role and organization. As Abhijit says, one's career journey is indeed a reflection of one's choices, opportunities and challenges. And as one moves from one chapter of their professional life to the next, how does one think of and define success? It is refreshing to read case studies from a variety of professional pursuits ranging from business to the creative sphere. And finally, the book also provides a relatable toolkit that readers can use readily to transform their careers for the better. The sketch notes provide a creative recap of the ideas'—**Aditya Ghosh, entrepreneur, founder, Homage and co-founder, Akasa Air**

'*Career 3.0* is a must-read for learning, HR and talent professionals in these disruptive and changing times. Abhijit Bhaduri takes a fresh look at careers in the age of AI, workplace shifts, shifting skills and new work-life balances.

'This provocative book focuses on six skills to future-proof your career: expertise building, storytelling, teaching readiness, navigating ecosystems, personal branding and a venture portfolio of skills. *Career 3.0* stretches the concept of 'career success' in a world where people may change their jobs ten times in a lifetime. It tackles the challenge and opportunities of coping with AI's impact on jobs, skills and competencies in one's career.

'Skill building will be imperative for a lifelong and rewarding career. This book shares a powerful and organic approach to continually building the next chapter of each employee's skills'
—**Elliott Masie, chair, Masie Learning Foundation**

'If, like me, you are constantly trying to learn how to unlearn and re-invent yourself for continued success in this fast-changing world, look no further than this book. In a simple, short and clear manner, my friend Abhijit has de-mystified the process of being successful and relevant well into your nineties and outlasting most of your employers, while having a fulfilling and rewarding career journey. Through delightful and pithy sketches, anecdotes from the lives of other multi-faceted and successful individuals and wisdom from his own vast, diverse and successful career, you will learn how to navigate the reality of today's 'skills economy'—where skills matter, not roles or jobs or titles'
—**Achal Khanna, CEO, the Society for Human Resource Management (SHRM), India, Asia Pacific and MENA**

'Abhijit Bhaduri's book *Career 3.0* is a must-read for anyone who wants to succeed in the fast-changing and unpredictable world of work. Through engaging and insightful stories of real people, he shows how to develop the skills of adaptability, learning and leadership that are essential for Career 3.0. This book is not only a riveting read, but also a practical handbook for navigating your career journey'—**Greg Satell, lecturer, Wharton School of Business, author of *Cascades* and *Mapping Innovation*, and contributor to *Harvard Business Review* and *Barron's***

'A must-read guide on how to reinvent yourself and future proof yourself: packed with riveting stories and actionable insights'—**Hayagreeva Rao, Atholl McBean Professor of Organizational Behavior, Graduate School of Business, Stanford University**

CAREER
3.0

Six Skills You *Must* Have
to Succeed

ABHIJIT BHADURI

PENGUIN
VIKING

An imprint of Penguin Random House

VIKING

USA | Canada | UK | Ireland | Australia
New Zealand | India | South Africa | China | Singapore

Viking is part of the Penguin Random House group of companies
whose addresses can be found at global.penguinrandomhouse.com

Published by Penguin Random House India Pvt. Ltd
4th Floor, Capital Tower 1, MG Road,
Gurugram 122 002, Haryana, India

First published in Viking by Penguin Random House India 2023

ISBN 9780670099641

Typeset in RequiemText by Manipal Technologies Limited, Manipal
Printed at Thomson Press India Ltd, New Delhi

www.penguin.co.in

To Nandini

If the path before you is clear,
you are probably on
someone else's

—*Joseph Campbell*

Contents

Introduction: Your Career Journey Is Your Fingerprint

Some people collect stamps. I collect stories, particularly stories about people's careers and how they unfolded.

Think about your career journey. How did you land up where you are currently? Was it a straight path or was it a series of strange coincidences and meetings with people? You have probably experienced your share of mean bosses and psychopaths as well as mentors who changed your life, besides the incredible twists and turns of fate that are a part of every career journey. Your career journey is shaped by a million factors that remain mostly unseen.

When I meet people, I try to find out how they made their choices and how their journey was shaped by factors beyond their control. Some people have great clarity about the work they want to do, while others discern their preferences over time.

Your career journey is like your fingerprint, unique and one of a kind. It's a reflection of the choices you make, the opportunities you seize and the challenges you overcome. Just as fingerprints are formed by the ridges and patterns on your fingertips, your career journey is formed by the experiences and people you encounter along the way.

An archetype is often described as a universal pattern found in stories, myths and legends, and can be applied to real-life situations. Think of it as a sort of 'model' that represents a certain type of person, idea or behaviour. Career paths follow three archetypes—Career 1.0, Career 2.0 and the emerging Career 3.0 that is likely to be the norm in the future.

The AI-Phone Moment—more work, fewer jobs

Careers lie at the intersection of three forces—work, workers and workplaces. The way work gets done determines the skills needed. The seller of a skill needs a buyer who is willing to pay for the skill or service. The marketplace brings the buyer and seller together. The organization is a marketplace that provides guaranteed regular payments (salary). The organization bundles different kinds of work and calls them jobs. A guaranteed job is called employment. A freelancer or an entrepreneur has to discover the marketplace where their skills will find a buyer. The employee does not need to look for work, the self-employed person does everyday. A career reflects the choices made over a lifetime to monetize skills, relationships and dreams.

The way work gets done has been changing. The Industrial Revolution was a big change in the way work was done. Then the discovery of electricity changed it further. Then came the computer, the Internet, high-speed Internet, better connectivity and the movement to the cloud; and each time the way we worked changed. The change was like an earthquake that happens in the plates of the earth. It is only when those giant waves reach the shore that we call it a tsunami. The world of work and careers is going through seismic shifts as we speak.

You may have heard of the iPhone Moment when a tectonic shift happened in the world of work. The falling price of data, faster connectivity, cheaper smartphones and a host of other factors combined to create this tectonic shift.

What we are witnessing now should be called the 'AI-Phone Moment'. We are witnessing that iPhone moment when artificial intelligence (AI) is changing the world of work. This is as profound a moment as the discovery of electricity. Humans will share their work, workforce and workplaces with AI. AI will be like electricity—invisible and everywhere. AI will change how we work.

Think of how the smartphone changed photography and what we expect of professional photographers. Everyone can now take good photographs thanks to smartphones. Professional photographers have to be visibly and substantially better to wow the viewers. Backed by AI, the smartphone has changed work (photography), the worker (the skills needed to be a photographer) and the marketplace for photography.

Generative AI (Gen AI) will change every kind of work as we know it. It is driving Hollywood artists to go on strike because AI-driven programs can create stunning screenplays, videos with voices and images based on commands written in the way we speak to each other. Gen AI will change almost every white-collar job and career.

Will criminals use Gen AI to create a dystopian world? Anything can be weaponized. A kitchen knife can create a chef and a murderer. The problem is not the weapon but the human using the tool. Gen AI is no different. As loopholes are found we will plug them.

We are increasingly moving away from lifetime employment and stable jobs to a world where specific skills will be needed. Anyone who has those skills will have work but may not be employed. Employers will build internal talent marketplaces to attract top talent. The line between what it means to be a freelancer and an employee will be blurred. People will alternate between the two multiple times.

The skills needed to be successful as an employee will be no different from those that self-employed professionals need. We will have to navigate a world where there is work but fewer jobs. Over the next few years, careers will move in uncharted and unknown directions the 'skills economy'.

The portfolio of skills we have will shape the opportunities for work. Employability will be dependent on skills that need to be continuously refreshed. The degrees and pedigree of the educational institution will become less important than the ability to learn and teach. As the 'half-life of skills' reduces (more on that later), career paths will be crafted based on a portfolio of skills and how they are used to solve problems. Declining fertility rates and greying populations will force governments to rethink policies about state-funded pensions, retirement and immigration. Employers will have to craft a reskilling and upskilling policy with the same precision as their product portfolio. The future will bring new and exciting career paths that we have never seen before.

Employers and governments across the world will try to delay paying out pensions because humans are living longer. France increased retirement from sixty-two to sixty-four years. UK is considering increasing it to sixty-seven to sixty-eight. wants to increase the pensionable age by two years. That has led to protests. Maybe they should have opted to start paying pensions only when they turn eighty because of demographic shifts. Over time, countries with ageing populations will have to rethink not just their pension schemes but also their policies around immigration, education, skilling and much more. Employers will not be able to buy their way out of a skill gap. It is the AI-Phone Moment for careers.

For the next few years, the country with the youngest population in the world will be India. It will become the talent pool for the world. This large talent pool needs to be absorbed through *a million new jobs to be created every month*. That is an impossible task for any government. Indian youth will have to rethink their career options very differently from the career models their forefathers have succeeded in.

The signs are everywhere. The 'creator economy' is taking root in the smaller towns and cities. Having a mobile phone and cheap data can create more career possibilities than an educational degree. This is why it is time to rethink how we will navigate our career across new opportunities and pathways.

A higher bar for being called an expert

AI-driven products such as ChatGPT will allow anyone to write great copy and marketing materials and create engaging presentations. Midjourney and DALL-E, both Gen AI model capable of generating images from textual descriptions, is redefining visual possibilities. Gen AI is writing code in multiple programming languages, and becoming a tool that is already improving the productivity of software engineers by 40 per cent. AI will change the way we work and set a higher bar in every field. Career opportunities will merge and fade away at a faster pace than what we are prepared for.

Creativity, adaptability, resilience and the ability to navigate human emotions will be the most prized abilities. The rules that drive the 'Creator Economy' will trickle into every job and every profession. Robot advisers are already managing high-frequency trading. Cars can self-park in impossibly tight parking spaces and drive themselves on busy motorways. Helplines are being managed by bots. The workforce of the world is now made up of humans and AI. Every student can have a tutor. Every teacher can have infinite teaching assistants who can grade tests and set quizzes, leaving the teacher with the task of motivating students to dream bigger dreams.

AI will do all the work that is complicated but rule-based, repetitive and at scale. The six skills that creators need to thrive in the creator economy will be valuable for self-employed creators as well as those who work for an employer. Each skill is connected to the other five. The combination is powerful.

Career 1.0 is the first career archetype. It is the traditional model of one skill based on the education one received. It is the usual three-stage career of learning, earning and retiring. Career 2.0 is about monetizing two skills in two different ecosystems. The skills of one ecosystem do not guarantee success in the other. Think of a doctor who is a musician (like Palash Sen of Euphoria). The skills are not portable across the two ecosystems—a hospital and entertainment.

Career 3.0 can be visualized like a pizza with each slice representing a unique skill that can be monetized. I have lived that life when I was self-employed. My revenue streams came from running an advisory firm, my keynotes, being coach and career strategist, a podcast and being a brand evangelist for Adobe and SHRM. I thrived in Career 3.0. In 2022, I jumped from Career 3.0 to Career 1.0 when Microsoft invited me to lead their global learning and development team. I have moved between the three archetypes. Career 3.0 is not the final level. Career choices reflect the constraints and possibilities that life has to offer.

Embracing and finding joy in your current work opens up pathways for fulfillment and satisfaction.

Six skills to future-proof your career

Whether you are an employee or a gig worker, these six skills will create opportunities at every stage of your career. The chief executive officer (CEO) of a corporation and the newbie entering the workforce will both need these six skills:

1. How to quickly build expertise in a field.
2. How to tell stories.
3. How to teach a skill online and build a community of learners.
4. How to become part of multiple ecosystems that are unique.
5. How to build a personal brand.
6. How to build a portfolio of skills and careers like a venture capitalist (VC).

As new ways of working emerge, new career paths will evolve. I hope this book will encourage you to take a moment to pause and reflect on the kind of choices you should make to thrive in the future.

This book is a collection of my lived experiences and the career stories of people I have coached and helped reinvent. Every story is real. Occasionally, I have changed the name and some information that reveals the identity of someone who wanted to stay anonymous.

I had the opportunity to coach Ravish Kumar (not his real name), a very successful actor from Bollywood. His unconventional looks made it hard to be cast as the lead actor in Hindi movies. He was a versatile actor and tried to make his way into regional cinema. As he turned fifty, he wanted to rethink his own career. He tried to reinvent himself as a motivational speaker but that was not very satisfying. I worked with him to help him rethink his career path. He experimented with a few options and eventually combined his love for food and acting. He started vlogging about every meal that he was eating. Sometimes it would be at a restaurant. Sometimes at a friend's home. His Instagram handle was on fire. The result was new revenue streams from YouTube and Instagram. That in turn got him back into Bollywood and beyond.

It's time to learn how to prepare for career paths that will last into our nineties and outlast most employers.

Abhijit Bhaduri
Email: abhijitbhaduri@live.com
Follow me on LinkedIn.com/in/abhijitbhaduri
and subscribe to my newsletter on LinkedIn

HAPPINESS OR SUCCESS

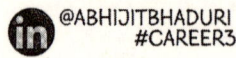

1

What Do You Want to Be When You Grow Up?

What do you want to be when you grow up?

This question always intrigued me because when I was a child, my answer kept changing ever so frequently. At the age of four, all I ever wanted to do was to have my pushcart to sell ice cream. When I said that, it always evoked laughter among the guests who came home. Then, I wanted to join the railways, inspired by my father, who spent his entire career working for one employer: the Government of India. A classic Career 1.0 role model.

But I was conflicted because I also wanted to be a doctor like my grandfather. I wanted to be a doctor and work in the railways.

'You could always become a doctor in the railways,' my father suggested. That reassured me for a while but also made me wonder if I was losing out by not exploring other ideas. At school, my friends would state their intention to become engineers and astronauts. Also, I met people who were lawyers and accountants. I began to see that there were many kinds of careers. One could be adventurous if one wanted to.

Career is our journey through life. As life happens, we must adapt to the new context. Ever changing career paths are built upon being flexible. It is the adaptable who can quickly change course, take risks and are prepared to fail.

Yes, being prepared to fail is what successful careers are built upon! Did I just use the word 'successful'?

What does it mean to be successful?

What is the measure of success in a career? How would you know that you have become successful? Alex Honnold became the first climber to scale the 3000-feet El Capitan rock in Yosemite, California, without a rope. He spent twenty years pursuing that dream. This high granite wall is 2.5 times as tall as the Empire State Building, or more than three times as high as the tip of the Eiffel Tower. Is he successful?

Who is the most successful soccer player ever? Would it be Pele? Messi? Ronaldo? What would be the criterion that one should use to compare their achievements? Their skill? Goals scored in the World Cup? The money they earned or donated? Their impact on the game?

Would Michael Phelps, with twenty-eight Olympic medals, qualify as the most successful sportsperson ever?

Who would you rate as the most successful actor?

Or the most successful doctor? That is hard to say.

Success is always relative. If you became the CEO of a company at forty you are successful until you meet the twenty-five-year-old CEO. Ryan Kaji is twelve and has a YouTube channel with 35.1 million subscribers. He made $30 million from his YouTube channel and $200 million from Ryan's world-branded toys and clothing.

Is he successful? His parents certainly think so!

It is very hard to decide the criteria that we must use to define success. Is it by earnings or by impact or by the challenges one has had to overcome to reach where one has?

How would you decide if you have been successful in your career? The truthful answer is that it is hard to do so. Every measure is debatable. No matter which success measure we use, there will be other yardsticks that will throw up a different answer. Success is always defined by others. Maybe we should measure success based on what one had to give up as a price for that success.

Why do rich people continue to work—even after they have made millions?

'The day I make my millions, I will quit working.'

Does this sound familiar?

I have worked with some rich and even mega-rich individuals and spoken to them at length. They continue to work punishing schedules, keep long hours, and travel continuously despite having millions or more stashed away. Several factors drive these individuals.

Some of them are passionate about their work and continue to do it because they love it. For example, successful entrepreneurs may continue to run their businesses because they are passionate about creating new products or solving their customers' problems.

Is your definition of success a 'thin' desire?

*Success is often measured by things like money, fame, or good grades. But these measures of success are often **thin desires**. They are influenced by what others want and can change quickly. For example, when someone orders something before you at a restaurant, if it usually makes you second-guess your original choice, you have fallen prey to a **thin desire**. If our career choices are driven by others, we may be limiting our potential.*

*Instead, it is important to focus on **thick desires**, which are deeply rooted in our own values and beliefs. By pursuing thick desires, we can find success that is meaningful and fulfilling to us.*

Success is a deeply personal and ever-changing concept. Take, for instance, Ernest Hemingway—a Nobel laureate in literature. His life was fraught with difficulties, and he ultimately took his own life in 1961. Similarly, Michael Jackson, the undisputed 'King of Pop', achieved dizzying heights of success in the music industry, but his personal life was mired in controversy, and he passed away at a young age. These examples illustrate that success is not a one-size-fits-all notion and that chasing it can be an exercise in futility. Success is often measured by external yardsticks that are subject to change. What truly matters is finding personal fulfilment and happiness, irrespective of societal definitions of success. Thick desires

> *generate the courage to make choices that make us happy. We must do an annual check-in to see if our choices are still meaningful to us. Try to evaluate your own definition of success. To understand if your definition of success and happiness. To understand if you definition is still fulfilling, consider these criteria: 1) Does it align with your personal values and beliefs? 2) Is your motivation internal or external? 3) Does it bring long-term fulfilment? By focusing on thick desires, you can find success that is meaningful and true to who you are.*

Several entrepreneurs and start-up founders continue to work hard despite hitting their financial goals because their start-up got bought over.

'Apart from being able to fund my hobby of getting a pilot's licence, my lifestyle has not changed,' said one founder who sold his startup to tech giant for millions.

Sometimes people hit their financial goals early because their stock options become valuable beyond imagination. That financial freedom may let them work for a company whose mission they believe in, but that may not pay enough.

A college student had once asked me, 'What is the point of earning money if you don't have an opportunity to spend it doing things that you like with people you care for?'

As careers continue to span more decades, people will have to rethink how they define their journey through life.

What makes people happy with their career choices?

Should you do what you love or love what you do? Having the autonomy to do a job the way one wants to, to do it well and be recognized as an expert and having the ability to make a difference to others have been the three biggest factors that make us happy.

It is often said that you should 'do what you love' when it comes to choosing a career. However, this advice can be misguided. Instead of focusing on finding a job that aligns with one's passions, it may be more practical to focus on finding a job that one can learn to grow to love. As one becomes more skilled in their work, they are more likely to be recognized as an expert in their field. This recognition can bring a sense of fulfilment and satisfaction, making it easier to love the work that one does. Additionally, becoming skilled in a particular field can open up new opportunities for growth and advancement, further increasing one's enjoyment of their work. In this way, it may be more beneficial to focus on loving what one does, rather than doing what one loves.

'Ultimately, one can learn to love their job if one is willing to put in the effort to become skilled and find fulfilment in their work.' This statement highlights the importance of effort and skill development in finding fulfilment in one's work. It is often easier to love what you do when you are good at it and feel a sense of accomplishment from your efforts. By focusing on developing your skills and becoming an expert in your field, you can increase your enjoyment of your work and find greater fulfilment in your career. Additionally, as you become more skilled, you may find that you have more autonomy and control over your work, which can also increase your enjoyment. In this way, it is often easier to love what you do by focusing on skill development and finding fulfilment in your work, rather than trying to find a job that aligns perfectly with your passions.

You can't and shouldn't be happy all the time

If you want success, focus on yourself. If you want happiness, focus on others. Talking of happiness, let me tell you about the research by Daniel Gilbert, one of the most influential researchers on happiness, a Harvard professor and the author of a book, *Stumbling on Happiness*. He says that you can't and shouldn't be happy all the time. If you were, you wouldn't value that happiness, and might even take it for granted.

1. Happiness does not come from setting and achieving goals. That feeling of happiness is synthetic and disappears quickly.
2. Happiness is not something that only the lucky few have.

Most people are unhappy about their careers.

Dan Gilbert's research provides simple tips to be happy and stay happy.

1. **Physical heath**: Being healthy makes you happy. Eating healthy, working out for thirty minutes a day, and getting seven hours of sleep are game changers.
2. **Healthy relationships**: Walk away from toxic relationships. Build better bonds with the people you love the most.
3. **Find time for fun**: Create a list of things that you like to do the most and prioritize them.

4. **Gratitude makes you happy**: Be thankful. For yourself, for your life, and for anything that gives you something, teaches you, or allows you to grow in any way.
5. **Find a reason to help someone every day**: Helping others can also make you happy.

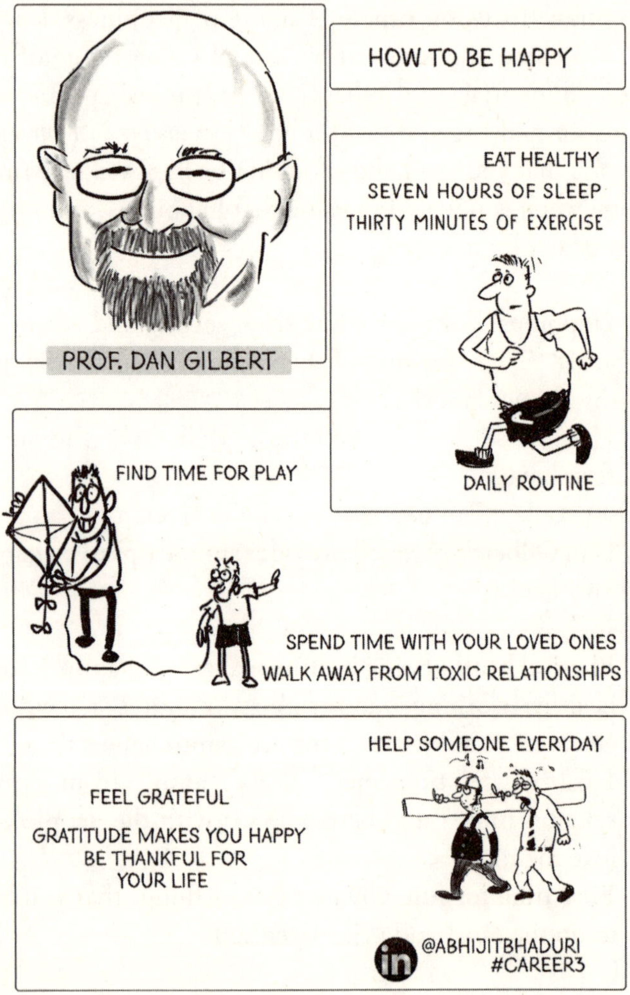

Dan Gilbert's career journey is equally fascinating. He went from being a high school dropout to a Harvard professor. Ask anyone to explain how they made their career choices, and you will hear about the role of chance, coincidences and the occasional lucky break that put them on the path to success or disappointment. Careers are shaped by a million factors.

Dan Gilbert—from high school dropout to Harvard professor

Can a high school dropout ever become a tenured professor at Harvard?

Today, Dan Gilbert is one of the most celebrated professors at Harvard. He dropped out of high school to spend a year driving around the country on a bus with a few friends. When the friends ran out of money, they would do odd jobs or simply ask someone to be charitable.

A year later, Dan Gilbert met a science fiction writer and tried to impress her by joining a course in writing at a small community college in the neighbourhood.*

The class was over-subscribed, and Dan Gilbert was offered the last seat in another course by the receptionist—a course titled 'Introduction to Psychology'.

---

* In the US, community colleges are usually public institutions providing continuing education. They offer courses that lead to certificates, diplomas and associate degrees. After graduating from a community college, some students transfer to a liberal arts college or university for two to three years to complete a bachelor's degree.

'Psychology can help me become a better writer,' he reasoned to himself and took it. The course showed him that there was a science to the things he had wondered about. His curiosity was kindled, and he kept taking one class after another in psychology.

The young Dan Gilbert now wanted to continue studying psychology. This was no casual exploration. He wanted to do a PhD in psychology. Because of his excellent scores in standardized testing, he was accepted at Princeton University. He is now called the 'Father of Positive Psychology' and his work has earned him worldwide fame and the opportunity to teach at Harvard University.

What if the seat available that afternoon had been in the cartography course instead of psychology?

'With the right professor, I would be a map maker,' says Dan Gilbert, without missing a beat.

Dan Gilbert, the erstwhile hippie and school dropout, puts it succinctly when he says,

'The distance is great, but the trajectory is clear.'

When asked what percentage of his life's goals he had accomplished, he replied, without hesitation, '172 per cent!'

Dan Gilbert's work on happiness is of relevance when it comes to choosing careers. While a certain amount of money does bring in rewards, beyond that, it is *social relationships that make us happy*. One of the most important beliefs this book endorses is that careers are built through relationships. It could mean someone taking a chance at an early stage of their career. It could sometimes mean that a stranger invited you to explore an opportunity that raised you out of career stagnation. It could mean the opportunity to make a difference at a scale you could never have achieved by yourself.

Why do some people come to hate a job they once dreamt of doing?

Vu started a restaurant in Manhattan. It had been his dream to bring authentic Vietnamese fast food to the city. The hours were brutally long. At night, Vu would be working till 10 p.m. cleaning up the kitchen and the tables, and tallying the cash register. He would sleep in the restaurant several days of the week so that he could receive the fresh vegetables and meat at 4 a.m. After three years of this routine, he shut down the restaurant because it was taking a toll on his mental health.

It was not a dream; it was a nightmare. Lack of work-life balance, too much or little stress and lack of opportunity to impact others are common reasons to hate a job that once seemed aspirational.

When there is constant and rapid change, the adaptable will thrive

Prof. Dan Gilbert's research on happiness says that we are poor predictors of our future state. We evolve as human beings and are continuously adapting to our circumstances and the world around us. In a world of constant change, it is the adaptable who will thrive.

Theoretically, we can find a perfect niche where we would be happy forever. Practically, that is unlikely because as our awareness of the world around us expands, our tastes evolve and so do our needs. The options that would have ranked in our top choices at age of fifteen are unlikely to be fulfilling a decade or two later.

If you were to get a childhood idol's name tattooed on your body, it could lead to embarrassment later in life. Another comparable situation is when researchers ask people who have eaten recently what and how much they would eat the following week. People always underestimate their appetites—because they are not hungry at that moment.

The same thing may happen to our career choices. Someone may become a doctor because they genuinely wish to help people get healthy. A few years later, there could be a nagging doubt that they could have made a better choice. On a bad day, one is highly likely to regret one's choices.

Pro tip: Talk to someone whose situation is similar to yours

Finding someone whose situation is similar to yours would mean finding broad similarities. While no two scenarios will be identical, there's a high possibility that someone's journey through life might be similar to yours.

'Studies indicate that you should ask others—"surrogates"—what they did in circumstances similar to what you are facing. That can be a powerful way to find solutions to get over temporary roadblocks. If your surrogate is happy about a particular choice, then you probably will be too. Asking an experienced surrogate is the most reliable and credible predictor of happiness and emotional satisfaction,' says Dan Gilbert in his book, *Stumbling on Happiness.*

You would imagine that people would find it easy to ask someone, who is already in a similar situation, what they like or dislike about their career choice. That would give them the ability to take an informed decision about how they would feel in the future. Most people believe that they are unique and have situations that have no parallels. They discount what 'surrogates' tell them. They assume that the surrogate's emotions and ideas are different from their own. In fact, the surrogate method works, because most human beings are alike.

In this book, we will delve into some of the forces that are shaping the future of careers, exploring the ways in which work is changing, the skills that will be most in demand, and the roles that companies and organizations will be looking to fill. We will examine the trends and predictions of experts in a variety of fields, from economics and technology to bartending and human resources, to paint a comprehensive picture of what the future of work might look like.

The advances in technology and automation have changed the way work gets done. As the nature of work changes, so do the skills that are required to succeed. Finally, the third factor is the employers themselves. The companies and organizations that are hiring will play a major role in shaping the careers of the future, as they seek out the workers with the skills and experience that are most valuable to them.

So, what does all of this mean for you and your career? The truth is that it's impossible to predict exactly what the future holds, but by understanding the trends and forces at play, you can make informed decisions about your own path. Whether you are just starting out in your career or are looking to make a change, this book will provide valuable insights and guidance as you navigate the complexities of the modern job market.

In the chapters that follow, we will explore several forces, examine the trends, study the predictions of experts and look at practical advice and strategies for success in the careers of the future. We will also delve into the broader social and economic context in which these trends are playing out and consider the ways in which they are likely to impact society as a whole.

So, if you are curious about the future of work and want to know what the next few decades might hold, this book is for you. Whether you are a student, a recent graduate, or a seasoned professional, the insights and advice contained within these pages will help you understand the forces that are shaping the future of careers and give you the tools you need to succeed in a rapidly changing world.

Let us start with a simple quiz.

Quiz: Some questions to help you think about your fit with a career archetype

Read the thirty sentences given below. They describe various preferences that we seek in our career. This is not a validated psychometric test. These are questions that let you think about your need for predictability, structure, risk-taking and learning something new constantly.

Tick seven sentences that describe the shape of your career choices.

1. Employers must assume responsibility to ensure that their employees have the skills to stay employable.
2. I may not always *want* to do something even if I am good at it.
3. A degree from a top-notch college and prior experience can guarantee career success.
4. I want to do something else even if I do not have a formal degree in it. I will teach myself.
5. I wonder whether this is the right time to try out an alternative career or if I should wait for a few more years.
6. I like clarity and structure because that is what will help build stability in my career.
7. I have friends from so many different professions, and I have often wondered if I could try out a couple of those professions just for fun.
8. I keep learning new skills even when there is no immediate use for that skill.
9. I do several short-term projects for other teams just to keep life interesting.
10. Promotions must be given on the basis of seniority because it encourages loyalty towards the employer.
11. Moonlighting and trying outside gigs is the best way to understand whether I can make a career switch today or whether I need to build my skills further.
12. My friends describe me as 'creative' and 'entrepreneurial'.

13. I am ready to give up what I have achieved to start chasing my dream job.

14. Promotions and financial rewards are the most effective ways to keep team members motivated.

15. We often regret what we have not had the courage to try. That is why I would rather try and fail if things don't turn out the way I think they should.

16. Uncertainty and constant change create so much stress that I am unable to focus on my job.

17. After retirement, I will not work for even a single day if I don't need the money.

18. Why should I retire at any age? There are a million things I want to try before I die.

19. I don't want to run away from my current job. I want to go towards the career that I want to build for myself.

20. There are some things I can do well and those are the things I stick to. I hate people who dabble in twenty different things. Just make up your mind, I'd like to tell them.

21. AI is going to create new career choices for every profession. What a fascinating time to be alive!

22. I am great at making friends with people who are completely unlike my close friends. I can live many lives through them.

23. A career path is best described as a ladder that you climb to reach the top of a mountain.

24. Life is too short to do just one thing for the rest of my life.

25. Should having 'family responsibilities' mean that I must stop dreaming?

26. AI is going to put so many people out of jobs. The government must formulate ways to prevent this.
27. Being a freelancer can give me more options to try and figure out where I can add value to others.
28. Weekends are reserved for building the skills I will need to succeed in my second career. That is the only way to turn it from a hobby to a main profession.
29. Money is not the only indicator of success. Having a second career gives me more ideas that I can bring into my day job.
30. A career path should be like taking a walk in a new city without a map. That is the only way you can meet new people, pause to look at something fascinating and maybe end up doing something completely different from what you planned to.

Scoring

There are ten sentences each that describe the three types of career paths. If all seven of your choices are in one category, then your preferences are clear. If your preferences are distributed between Career 1.0, 2.0 and 3.0, then reading this book will offer you clarity about how to proceed further.

Career 1.0:

1, 3, 6, 10, 14, 16, 17, 20, 23, 26

If you said yes to six or more statements in this category, you may have found the stability that you want in your career. You love to be the specialist or deepen your skills in the field you have chosen. Finding opportunities to do more in this field will mean continuously building your skills to be at the cutting edge of your profession.

Career 2.0:

2, 4, 5, 11, 13, 15, 19, 25, 28, 29

You have a day job that you can do and probably do well. It is not what you have always dreamt of doing and this is a temporary phase you must endure. You have nurtured your passion over the years and want to make it your main career choice. You may have wondered if your dream job can also provide financial stability and the recognition you need. There are already lots of people doing what you have been planning to. You wonder whether this is the right time to take the plunge.

Career 3.0:

7, 8, 9, 12, 18, 21, 22, 24, 27, 30

You have a curious mind and are receptive to interesting possibilities. You are constantly thinking about career choices that you can explore. You have a high degree of learning agility and have very strong people skills. Maybe you spend your weekends learning about a new skill even when there is no apparent use for what you are learning. You often wonder what you would study if you went back to college today or even five years later? You have taken risks in your career and some of those moves may have worked out for you. You wonder how some people can do just one thing their entire life. That is not for you because life is too short, and you want to try out everything that you can. If anyone wrote about your career, that book would be titled 'Many Lives, Many Masters'.

Some pointers to keep in mind

(i)   Career 2.0 is not better than Career 1.0 or worse than Career 3.0. People will juggle all types of archetypes.
(ii) Our career paths are shaped by several factors and as a result, there are always opportunities to make different choices.
(iii) Our career path will be uniquely our own shaped by skills, our ability to learn, work with others and risk-taking ability.
(iv) There are phases where our choices may be shaped by factors beyond our control and there will be phases when we can exercise our will.
(v)   Most people will move in and out of these three archetypes multiple times during their lifetime.

Let us get started.

2

What Does Career Success Mean to You?

More than 1,500 people were asked, 'What does career success mean to you?'*

This is what they said:

a. Being financially independent: 50 per cent
b. Interesting projects: 11 per cent
c. Being promoted faster than peers are: 4 per cent
d. Creating long-lasting value: 35 per cent

---

* Bhaduri, Abhijit, 'What does success mean to you?', n.d., LinkedIn, https://www.linkedin.com/posts/abhijitbhaduri_career-successs-careersuccess-activity-7014420884828397568-sjvR/, accessed on 3 October 2023.

Career paths are like mountain streams. They flourish in the monsoon and are down to a trickle in the summer. Sometimes the streams rush along, jumping over stones and obstacles. At other times, the stream carves a new path to go around a seemingly insurmountable challenge.

Think of your career journey as a mountain stream. Have a broad direction you want to move towards, but don't fix a time bound target (e.g., become vice president [VP] by age X). Be open to change, realignments and resetting your priorities.

According to a recent study, the average person changes jobs ten times in their lifetime. However, this number can vary depending on a number of factors such as age, education and work experience.*

There are many factors driving the trend towards multiple careers. Advancements in technology, changes in the economy, and shifts in societal values can all contribute to changes in the job market. Additionally, people may choose to change careers for personal reasons such as a desire for new challenges or a better work-life balance. Every time someone asked me, 'What do you want to be when you grow up?' I wish I had said, 'I just want to be happy when I grow up.'

---

* Cathie, 'How Many Career Changes Will the Average Person Experience in their Lifetime?' List Foundation, December 31, 2021, https://www.listfoundation.org/how-many-career-changes-will-the-average-person-experience-in-their-lifetime, accessed on August 4, 2023.

The changing work-worker-workplace equation shapes your career choices

CAREERS ARE SHAPED BY CHANGES IN ANY OF THESE

HOW **WORK** GETS DONE

FREE FOOD JOIN ME

HIRING NOW

JOIN US   JOIN US

WORKPLACES
ABILITY TO ATTRACT
THE PEOPLE WITH SKILLS

AI

SUPPLY & DEMAND
OF SKILLS IN THE
WORKFORCE

@ABHIJITBHADURI
#CAREER3

There are three key factors that shape our careers: the way work is done, the supply and demand for skills and the workplace as a marketplace for skills.

(i) **How work gets done**: The way work is done can be thought of as a trend. Whether it's steam, electricity, or AI plus humans, it's what's current. Every sector and industry is using AI to create new competitive moats. Humans will lose their jobs not to AI but to humans using AI. Similarly, firms using AI will replace firms that are not using AI.

(ii) **The skills to do the work**: The demand for skills change constantly. Did you know that the word 'talent' originally referred to a unit of weight used for weighing precious metals? Over time, it came to refer to special natural abilities or gifts. The market for every skill is shifting. A skill that is sought after today may not find a mention in your resume tomorrow as you keep learning. If your resume does not reflect new skills every year, it is time to rethink your career strategy.

(iii) **The marketplace for skills**: Workplaces are marketplaces for skills. Opportunities in a rapidly growing start-up will be different from a well-established large firm. Choosing the right marketplace can be powerful way to shape our career. Changing the workplace could mean changing the country or sector or employer or going remote. Each variable can change the career trajectory. Choose the marketplace where your skills are valued the most.

Changes in how we work: With the advent of steam power and later electricity, many jobs became easier and safer, as machines could handle much of the heavy lifting and hazardous tasks. Historically, the change in work happened first. That triggered the change in the workforce. The workplace then made rules and systems to hold the workforce together.

As technology advanced, computers became an increasingly important tool in the workplace. At first, computers were mainly used for tasks like data entry and analysis, but as they became more powerful, they started to take on more complex tasks. This led to the rise of careers in computer science and information technology, as people with expertise in these fields were in high demand to design, build and maintain the systems that were driving the modern economy.

Today, we are seeing another major shift in the way work is done, as Gen AI becomes increasingly prevalent in the workplace. AI has the potential to revolutionize every industry, automating and augmenting tasks that were previously done by humans and allowing us to work more efficiently and effectively.

However, this shift also poses challenges, as most jobs may change as AI takes over certain tasks. Even the people whose skills are currently valued will have to learn new skills. Ability to learn will matter more than previous experience or even a formal degree.

One example of how AI is changing the way we work is in the field of customer service. Many companies are now using Gen AI and other AI-powered systems to handle basic customer inquiries and complaints, freeing up human customer service representatives to focus on more complex and high-level issues. This allows companies to provide better service to their customers while reducing their labour costs. It is giving rise to the demand for 'prompt engineering'—the prompt that lets ChatGPT be most impactful. AI experts have already found that people with degrees in literature and philosophy are better than software engineers at writing prompts. Our assumptions about career choices will be challenged every day.

AI is also being used in industries like healthcare, finance and manufacturing to automate tasks and improve efficiency. For example, AI algorithms can analyse medical records and help doctors identify patterns and make more accurate diagnoses. In finance, AI can be used to analyse market trends and help investors make more informed decisions. And in manufacturing, AI is being used to optimize production processes and identify potential problems before they occur.

As AI gets embedded in every piece of software, it will become the invisible power that will change how we work. With each keystroke of the user, the software will learn about the user and personalize the offering. Your streaming service can already predict the movies you will like. Digital maps can predict your journey time and provide alternative routes if you miss a turn. While AI has the potential to change the way we work in many industries, it's important to remember that it will also create new career opportunities. As AI becomes more prevalent, there will be a need for professionals who have expertise in areas like machine learning, data science and natural language processing. It will create new opportunities in every sector and for every kind of work that is done. We will live in a world where there will be plenty of work for everyone but not enough jobs and limited options for lifetime employment.

Changes in the workforce: The talent pool reflects the skills that people have and the demand for that skill. The demand and supply of skills can shape careers. The demand for a skill can be triggered by many factors. From wars, famine and technology to the laws and regulations, the demand for skills changes like the waxing and waning phases of the moon.

Climate change and rising temperatures across the world will drive people away from work that requires working in the sun. Farming may not be an attractive career. Construction activity will have to be done at night to avoid the daytime heat. Climate change can shape the demand and supply of the talent pool.

So does crime. Cybersecurity is a rapidly evolving field that requires professionals to constantly adapt to new threats and challenges. As cybercriminals, including hackers and state-sponsored actors, become more sophisticated in their methods, the demand for skilled cybersecurity professionals increases. This can create new opportunities for professionals with the right skills and expertise to protect against these threats. In this way, even criminal activity can drive changes in the job market and make certain skills more valuable. The increasing interconnectivity of systems, such as the Internet of Things (IoT), creates additional vulnerabilities that need to be addressed through cybersecurity measures. As governments and industry organizations implement new regulations and policies to address cybersecurity risks, organizations may need to hire professionals to ensure compliance with these regulations.

With a rise in the ageing population of the world, people who have the skills to address the needs of this population will be highly valued. That could mean that every skill from financial advisers to healthcare to assistive technology will grow. We will need to find ways to tap into new talent pools like refugees and immigrants and even retired people who will need to be reskilled.

Having a skill that will grow in demand is a smart way to choose a career. What is the best way to find out which skills will be in demand? What seems to be in demand today may not be valued by the time one gets the degree or certification. The supply and demand for skills is constantly changing and with it, the available career options.

We are moving away from a world where a degree came with a lifetime warranty. The employers have been complaining about the dropping rates of employability. As the demand and supply of skills fluctuate at a dizzying rate, being able to learn new skills will be necessary for everyone. But being able to teach others will be even more valuable.

Reskilling eight billion people continuously is a problem all of us have to solve together.

Changes in the workplace: Every workplace is marketplace for skills. Think of continuous updating of skills like the way the apps on your phone get updated every couple of days. In a poll on LinkedIn, 42 per cent of the respondents said that they were doing their own skill building. Only 14 per cent of the respondents said that their learning was driven by their employers.[*] This may be the weak signal that employers must listen to. Workplaces are not helping employees continuously keep their skills current. Investing in self-driven learning must be followed by coaching and mentoring done by the team leaders or people managers. Having the opportunity to work in projects that span a few weeks to a few months is what every employer must do. Investing in skill development is the smartest talent management strategy for the future.

---

[*] Bhaduri, Abhijit, 'How has your approach to learning and development changed in the last 12 months', n.d., LinkedIn, https://www.linkedin.com/posts/abhijitbhaduri_learning-development-online-activity-7082439006096908288-j5pn.

By 2050, people aged sixty-five and older will make up nearly 40 per cent of the population in some parts of East Asia and Europe. Aging rich countries will need to rethink pensions, immigration policies and what life in old age looks like. Changing the pensionable age in France led to massive protests. Political parties find it easy to paint a picture of immigrants taking away jobs. Demographic shifts will drive more fundamental changes in career opportunities than ever before.*

The workplace continuously designs incentives that matter to the people it is trying to attract. This system is driven not just by tangible things like compensation and benefits but also by intangible elements like the leadership team, the calibre of the talent working there and the culture that binds it together. A positive and supportive work culture promotes collaboration, communication and respect among employees.

Policies that prioritize work-life balance and offer flexible work arrangements, paid time off, and other support to help employees maintain a healthy balance between their professional and personal lives are becoming valuable to attract talent across sectors.

Today, workplaces are also rethinking ways to engage talent in a variety of engagement formats beyond full-time employment. These formats are short-term projects, part-time roles, job-sharing, gig workers, hackathons and many other options to be part of a workplace. This has a

---

* Leatherby, Lauren, 'How a Vast Demographic Shift Will Reshape the World', *New York Times*, July 25, 2023, https://www.nytimes.com/interactive/2023/07/16/world/world-demographics.html, accessed on July 2, 2023.

significant impact on career paths. Kathleen Hogan, the chief people officer and executive vice president, human resources of Microsoft, refers to 5Ps: Pay, Perks, People, Pride and Purpose that must come together. 'A deep sense of Purpose, combined with Pay, Perks, People and Pride, is where the magic happens,' she says.

WHAT MAKES FOR A GREAT WORKPLACE

PEOPLE   PAY AND PRIDE

PERKS   PURPOSE

@ABHIJITBHADURI
#CAREER3

3

Three Career Archetypes

Career 1.0: Monetizing a single skill in one ecosystem

In Career 1.0, individuals are focused on monetizing a single skill that they have developed through training or experience. This may be a skill that they have formally studied or learned through on-the-job experience. Stable workplaces with relatively few changes offer opportunities for a person to continue pursuing a career with a single employer or doing the same work for different employers. Professional sports is a good example of Career 1.0 where a single skill is monetized in one ecosystem as the rules of a game don't really change. A professional singer spends a lifetime using one skill in one ecosystem.

TRADITIONAL
CAREER PATHS
HAVE FOLLOWED
THIS THREE STAGE
APPROACH:
LEARN, EARN & RETIRE

@ABHIJITBHADURI
#CAREER3

There are a few key characteristics that define Career 1.0:

Specialization: Individuals in Career 1.0 tend to specialize in a specific skill or area of expertise. This allows them to differentiate themselves from others in their field and become known as experts in their area of focus.

Deep knowledge: To monetize their skill effectively, individuals in Career 1.0 need to have a deep understanding of their area of expertise. This may involve continuous learning and staying up to date with the latest developments in their field.

Limited flexibility: One of the drawbacks of monetizing a single skill is that it can limit flexibility. For example, if an individual has developed expertise in a specific software programme, they may struggle to pivot to a different area of work if that software becomes outdated or if they are unable to find work using that skill. A sportsperson may find it difficult to switch from one sport to another.

Career 2.0: Monetizing a second skill in two unique ecosystems

TWO CAREER PATHS DRIVEN
BY TWO DIFFERENT SKILLS   @ABHIJITBHADURI
                                        #CAREER3

In Career 2.0, individuals are monetizing a second skill, in a distinctly different ecosystem. This second skill may be something that they have formally studied or have been trained in, or it may be a skill that they have developed through personal interests or hobbies. A college professor who writes a bestselling book or the CEO who serves on the board of a start-up is operating in a second ecosystem. The skills gained in an ecosystem may not be useful to succeed in the second ecosystem. That is no different from the accountant who performs as a stand-up comedian on weekends or the coder who drives an Uber to make a few extra bucks. They are all using a second skill, in a new ecosystem in a Career 2.0 model. Monetization is proof of proficiency and a buyer who finds your skill valuable.

There are a few key characteristics that define Career 2.0:

Diversification: Monetizing a second skill allows individuals to diversify their income streams and reduce their risk of financial vulnerability. This can be especially useful in times of economic uncertainty or if there is a drop in the demand for an individual's primary skill.

Flexibility: Monetizing a second skill can also increase flexibility, as it gives individuals time to pivot to a different area of work. The relationships in every ecosystem creates new career pathways.

Time management: Managing two skills simultaneously can be challenging, as it requires careful time management and the ability to juggle multiple tasks. It may also involve making trade-offs and sacrifices in order to prioritize one skill over the other.

Relationships: Building a network in a different ecosystem requires people to be adaptive. Being able to sense and then adapt oneself to the dynamics and power play in two different ecosystems is a skill that needs to be nurtured. Being able to meet people from different professions is a great way to start learning about the opportunities the field offers. It is easy to become an apprentice to practitioners in the field and learn new skills in a practical way.

Career 3.0: Monetizing three or more skills in different ecosystems

In Career 3.0, individuals are monetizing three or more skills in different ecosystems. I once met an accountant who works for a large multinational corporation (MNC).

He spends his weekends cooking for a restaurant in the neighbourhood whose customers love his curries and cakes. He also plays the keyboard and drums and used to play for a band when he was a student. The band were so successful that for a while he thought of doing that full-time. Laughing, he adds, 'My problem is that I enjoy being an accountant as much as I enjoy being a chef and a musician. Why limit myself?'

Paychex, an American firm providing human resources services, found in a survey that 40 per cent of workers in the US have multiple jobs, and half of Gen Z workers are splitting their time between three or more employers. They call it 'polyworking'. Meanwhile, 33 per cent of millennials are holding down three or more jobs, compared to 28 per cent of baby boomers and 23 per cent of Gen X professionals.[*]

There are a few key characteristics that define Career 3.0:

Curiosity: Career 3.0 comes naturally to people who are curious. They will often experiment and learn something new just to be able to figure it out. They teach themselves by watching videos, listening to experts, finding apprenticeships and attending classes. Most of all the learning by being unafraid of failure. When an opportunity

---

[*] Royle, Orianna Rosa, 'Gen Zers Are Now "Polyworking" Because Holding down Just One Job Doesn't Pay Enough or Give Them the Flexibility They Want', *Fortune*, March 20, 2023, https://fortune.com/2023/03/20/gen-z-polyworking-one-job-not-pay-enough-flexibility-paychex/, accessed on August 4, 2023.

comes their way, they are often prepared to grab it. These are people who are comfortable with skills that are often seen to be at two ends of a spectrum—e.g., science and coding both demand logic and are polar opposites of fields like humanities and languages. Curious people often enjoy learning something even though there is no apparent use for it. Quiz contests often bring together people who are curious about everything from Greek mythology to astronomy to sports.

Adaptability: Monetizing multiple skills requires adaptability, as individuals may need to shift between different areas of work depending on the demands of each skill. Being comfortable with ambiguity and being flexible go together. An unpredictable world that is constantly evolving needs people who are comfortable with uncertainty. It is much like driving through thick fog. The driver keeps going despite the low visibility.

Mindset: Career 3.0 needs the mindset of a VC who has to quickly figure out whether the idea being pitched is a big idea that has potential—an opportunity they must not miss, or if it is a passing fad. It often means that the VC has to place multiple bets knowing that the majority of the investments will fail but that the one that succeeds will more than make up for the rest. It needs the ability to take risks and walk on a path less travelled.

Overall, the three career archetypes—Career 1.0, Career 2.0, and Career 3.0—represent different approaches to monetizing skills and building a career. While each approach has its own benefits and drawbacks, the key is to find the right balance that works for an individual's unique strengths and goals.

Career 1.0, Career 2.0 and Career 3.0 are not rigid boundaries

Career opportunities are shaped by changes in the way work is performed. For example, if job applicants can use the power of AI to write their curriculum vitae (CVs), then it will change the way hiring is done. The demand and supply of skills can create or kill career paths. Careers in oceanography may involve research or data collection skills. The tiny country of Estonia has already transformed the way a nation serves people beyond its borders through e-Residency. Now with the Digital Nomad Visa, Estonia is transforming how people in the world choose to work.

Career 1.0 has been the most common traditional career archetype where there is one source of monetization. In Career 2.0, a second skill gets monetized. The third archetype is Career 3.0 where three or more skills are being monetized.

In Career 1.0, the work being done, the skills that are needed and the workplace remain relatively stable and unchanged. In Career 2.0, the second gig can be created by a second kind of work—a side gig, that needs a different skill and is practised in a different workplace.

Sarah Cooper worked in design for Yahoo! and in user experience for Google Docs, Sheets, and Slides while also performing stand-up comedy. Cooper left Google to focus full-time on writing and comedy. Her observations about the absurdities of the workplace appeared in a book called

100 Tricks to Appear Smart in Meetings. It was published in 2016 and became a bestseller and helped her rise to fame as a stand-up comedian. She is also known for her funny TikTok videos. She is a keynote speaker, a stand-up comedian and author and a star on social media. She also has a show on Netflix. Career 3.0 is the emerging archetype as the lifespan of a skill becomes as short as our attention span.

Career 3.0 can happen because of multiple skills create multiple income streams.

1. **A new workplace**: Every new skill cannot necessarily be monetized. In case of teachers, when they offer private tuitions after school or college, it is a second source of income, but it is the same skill being used in a different ecosystem. Instead of teaching the students in school or college, teaching them in a different workplace (eg. online tutoring) could open new career possibilities.
2. **A new skill—an adjacent skill**: Adjacent skills refer to skills that are closely related or connected to a particular skill or area of expertise. These skills often complement and enhance a person's existing knowledge and abilities and may be related to the same industry or field of work. For example, if someone is a software developer, their adjacent skills might include programming languages such as Python or Java, as well as database management or data analysis. These skills are related to software development but are not necessarily part of the core skill set of a software developer.
3. **A different career path using new skills**: Signing up to do a new course whether in college, at the employers'

or at a training firm is a common practice for people to build skills. Some educational institutions offer dual degrees to people and that opens a new career path possibility. Some people may pick up skills later in life by being an apprentice to someone, creating new skills and new prospects.

'As of August 2020, I've been a doctor in the UK for two years, and I'm now taking a one-year sabbatical from medicine to explore my other interests,' says Ali Abdal, who describes himself as 'a YouTuber, podcaster, ex-doctor, and soon-to-be author'. Ali Abdaal is a UK-based entrepreneur, YouTuber, podcaster, and ex-doctor. He is known for sharing productivity tips, practical life advice, and strategies for living happier, healthier, and more productive lives on his YouTube channel that has more than two million subscribers.

Case: Mitali

I spoke to Mitali (not her real name) who changed from being a teacher to taking up a second career as a content creator.

'As a young woman fresh out of college, I always knew that I wanted to be a teacher. There was just something about the idea of shaping young minds and helping students grow and learn that really appealed to me. After graduation, I was lucky enough to land a job at a small elementary school. I spent long hours grading papers, planning lessons, and building relationships with my students. Some parents requested me to offer private tuition. I loved every minute of it, and I could see the difference I was making in the lives of my students. I even got approached by the local coaching centre, but I did not like that environment and said, 'No.''

'I think word got around and my principal asked me if I would like an opportunity to expand my skills and get paid to do that. She asked if I would do an additional role as a coach and offered to double my salary. I started coaching the school's basketball team. This meant more money, but I was really motivated by the work. I also became a mentor to newer teachers, offering support and guidance as they navigated their own careers.

'After several years as a teacher, I was offered the position of principal. It was a big step up in my career, and I was excited about the opportunity to make a difference on a larger scale. However, I quickly found that administrative work took up a lot of my time and energy, leaving me little time for the things that I enjoyed. I had been dazzled by the position and regretted my choice.

'To cope with the stress of my new role, I turned to cooking to relax and unwind. I found that I really enjoyed experimenting with new recipes and tried out some of my grandmother's recipes. I was struck by how much I had forgotten about these dishes and how much I missed them. I was never as good as Ammu but close enough to pass off as a good follower!

I decided to start writing down her recipes. I spent hours in the kitchen, testing and perfecting the recipes, and I began to dream of publishing a cookbook. After much hard work and determination, I finally approached a publisher with my idea. To my surprise, they were interested and offered me an advance to complete the project.

'As I worked on the project, I began to wonder if I might have a future as a full-time author. When the book was finally released, I was thrilled to see it do so well. As part of the promotion for the book, my publisher asked me to start a YouTube channel to share some of the recipes and cooking techniques that I had used in the book.

My YouTube channel gained a considerable following, and I started getting some money from advertisers. Prior to this, I had not known that one could get paid to put videos on one's channel. I began to see it as a new source of income to offer scholarships to some students. As my followers grew, I realized that I had stumbled upon a third career path that I was truly passionate about. I continue to teach and lead as a principal, but I also now consider myself a full-time author and YouTube creator. It's been an incredible journey, and I'm grateful for all the experiences and opportunities that have come my way.'

The impact of the 'Creator Economy' on the future of careers

The 'Creator Economy' describes the class of businesses built by over fifty million independent content creators, curators, and community builders including social media influencers, bloggers and videographers, plus the software and finance tools designed to help them with growth and monetization.[*]

The Creator Economy is the new disruptor that is the main driving force behind the Career 3.0 archetype. It is a new and rapidly growing sector of the economy that is driven by the rise of social media, online platforms, and other digital technologies. It is characterized by a decentralized, networked model of production and distribution, in which individuals and small groups create and share content, products and services online.

Goldman Sachs research expects the fifty million global creators to grow at a 10–20 per cent compound annual growth rate during the next five years. Creators earn income primarily through direct branding deals to pitch products as an influencer; via a share of advertising revenues with

---

[*] Yuan, Yuanling, and Josh Constine, 'SignalFire's Creator Economy Market Map', Signalfire (blog), https://signalfire. com/creator-economy/, accessed July 16, 2023.

the host platform; and through subscriptions, donations and other forms of direct payment from followers. Driven by better connectivity, easy access to hardware and software, multiple platforms that are AI-powered, the creator economy is expected to be a half a trillion-dollar opportunity by 2027.[*]

The traditional media houses are no longer the only option to go live on. Anyone with a mobile phone can post a ten-second video or a long movie on YouTube, Instagram, Facebook or even on their own website, without requiring any approvals from editors or any other kinds of gatekeepers.

This is true for every form of creative content. Authors, painters, stand-up comedians, acrobats and many others are thriving in this creator economy. Online classes, art, music, fitness, podcasts and videos are all possible opportunities for building an audience that leads to monetization through:

a) Courses—there are several platforms that support creators who want to launch their own courses
b) Non-Fungible Tokens
c) Brand endorsements
d) Live shopping
e) Fashion marketplaces
f) Fan interactions

---

[*] Goldman Sachs, 'The Creator Economy Could Approach Half-a-Trillion Dollars by 2027,' n.d., https://www.goldmansachs.com/intelligence/pages/the-creator-economy-could-approach-half-a-trillion-dollars-by-2027.html, accessed on August 4, 2023.

Some of these formats will be temporary opportunities. Others will endure the test of time. There is no denying the range of possibilities that exists today. Popular creators can now start offering their content on their own website or on a digital format of their choosing. They start by seeking audience engagement on traditional digital platforms like YouTube, TikTok, Facebook, Instagram etc. They can very quickly turn this into the freemium model where there are two versions of the same format, one available for free and the other paid for.

The availability of free or reasonably priced software allows creators to edit their audio-video content in a manner that only professionals working in studios were able to earlier. Smartphones make it possible to shoot high-quality videos and even edit them on the fly before they are posted to millions of fans hungry for content.

The Creator Economy is rewriting the rules around the way we work; these rules will shape careers in the future. In the past, careers were often based on long-term employment with a single employer, and advancement was based on seniority and merit. In the Creator Economy, careers are more fluid and dynamic, and success is often based on an individual's ability to create and share value online.

The rise of the creator economy has opened new opportunities for individuals to create their own careers and be their own boss. It has also created challenges, as the lack of traditional employment and benefits can make it difficult for creators to earn a stable income and secure long-term financial security.

One key factor that will shape careers in the creator economy is the ability to build and engage an audience that is online. In the past, a strong network of personal and professional contacts was important for career advancement, but in the Creator Economy, a large and engaged online following can be even more valuable. Creators who can build a strong brand and consistently produce high-quality content that resonates with their audience are more likely to succeed in the Creator Economy.

Another important factor is the ability to adapt and learn new skills quickly. The Creator Economy is constantly evolving, and successful creators are those who can stay up to date with new trends and technologies and learn new skills as needed. This may involve investing in formal education or training, or simply being proactive about staying informed and learning on the job.

In addition to these skills, successful creators know how to communicate their value proposition to their audiences. They are also able to effectively manage their time and resources and can balance the demands of creating content with other aspects of their lives. The world is changing at an unprecedented rate, and such changes bring shifts in the way we work, the skills that are in demand, and the very nature of the jobs we hold. The future of careers is a topic that is on the minds of many people as they consider their own paths and try to navigate an increasingly complex and rapidly evolving job market.

4

Did I Choose the Right Career?

And how to be happy with your choices

I am always jealous of people who knew exactly what they wanted to do in their life. They are self-assured and are never plagued by self-doubt the way I am. I am no spring chicken. I have spent several decades working in a range of companies in India and abroad. I have worked across sectors and even switched from being a specialist to a generalist and then back to being a specialist.

I try to keep self-doubt from my mind, but it keeps buzzing around like an annoying insect you are trying to keep away as you focus on the ice cream. Have you, like me, wondered, 'Did I choose the right career? Should I have chosen a different stream to graduate in? Did I make a mistake in grabbing the first opportunity that came my way? Did I let other people and their successes influence me disproportionately? Should I have listened to my heart when it was trying to whisper something to me?'

Just about anything can trigger these questions in my mind. It can happen when things are going well, and it is more likely when things are not. When I see a peer moving ahead (in my field or in another organization), these questions resurface in my mind. When someone gets a promotion or a better increment, I'm completely convinced I must know the answer to that question. What makes it worse is that even when everything is going well and there is no reason to complain, there is still that nagging doubt, 'Is it too late to switch and do something else now?'

Sometimes the trigger can be a harmless piece of news I come across while mindlessly scrolling down my smartphone. That is what happened the other day when I read about the rising cases of myopia in the world.

More than 80 per cent of the population of Singapore, South Korea, Taiwan and China need spectacles to see objects at a distance. Half the world's population will be short-sighted by 2050. That means four billion people could potentially need glasses. Short-sightedness or myopia is on the rise. People are spending more time reading and less time outdoors looking at objects in the distance. Houses are smaller and we are all watching television or squinting at our smartphones. Adults are spending time on video calls. Gaming is on the rise, and we are watching YouTube videos to learn, entertain ourselves and connect with others through screens.

Increasing levels of literacy is a goal every government is chasing. The by-product is career opportunities for those trying to fix the problem of myopia across the globe.[*]

This is a great time to become an optometrist or an ophthalmologist, to open a shop to sell eyewear, to manufacture corrective lenses, to join a start-up offering eye testing as a service or become an eyewear designer. There will be a huge demand for professors who can teach students about glaucoma, retinal detachment, cataract, and myopic maculopathy. These are all problems affecting adults and even children at an alarming pace. Short-sightedness is a problem that affects the rich. They will need to wear glasses. So fancy designer eyewear is going to thrive as a business. Then there will be people who do not like to wear glasses and will opt for contact lenses. That means a never-ending demand for ophthalmologists, optometrists and licensed opticians.

Do I have what it takes to pursue a career as an ophthalmologist? Or would I be more successful selling eyewear? Is it too late to think of a career switch and ride this wave? Should I pursue it on the side?

In 2020, two-fifths of the world's population was overweight or obese. By 2035, a staggering four billion people could be classified as overweight or obese. People everywhere are getting fatter. The populations putting on pounds the fastest are not in the rich West but in countries

---

[*] Mudditt, Jessica, 'Why Short-Sightedness Is on the Rise', BBC, 5 October 2022, https://www.bbc.com/future/article/20220927-can-you-prevent-short-sightedness-in-kids, accessed 16 July 2023.

like Egypt, Mexico and Saudi Arabia. Dieting and weight loss is a $250-billion industry. I wonder if I would be better off fighting obesity or correcting vision.

Someone told me that they wanted to be a 'Master Cicerone'—that is, an expert in beer. There are barely two dozen people in the world who are certified as Master Cicerones. According to the *Economist*, in 1982, there were just ninety-three breweries in the USA. Now there are almost 10,000 of them. That could be a fun job to do. I could drink beer all day and it would be considered work! With all the chatter about AI, it is not surprising that a new career opportunity as 'prompt engineer' has already been created. What is needed is an educational qualification to support it. Could that be a career for me?*

Then the alarm bell rings, and I wake up with the horrible realization that I am late for work. I go to the office and promise myself that I will explore these career options later.

I can tell you that I had no idea what I would do when I grew up. My maternal grandfather was a doctor, and a very successful one at that. For a very long time I would tell people that I would become a doctor like *Dadu*. The reality was that I never enjoyed studying science. I enjoyed studying English and had even published a few short stories in the school magazine. When it came to choosing which subject I knew it would not be science. The problem was

---

* 'Lol. First Companies in Germany Hire "Prompt Engineers"', Reddit, 8 February 2023, https://www.reddit.com/r/ StableDiffusion/comments/10wci46/lol_first_companies_ in_germany_hire_prompt/, accessed 16 July 2023.

that the school did not have enough students opting for the humanities and hence did not offer the option. So, I had to study commerce and really hated it. In college, I studied economics and then went on to pursue an MBA. After that, I started my journey through corporate India. I did a bachelor's degree in law because a few friends told me that they were doing it. Judge me if you will, but I will confess that I had no specific reason to study law. I did not even want to be a lawyer. My choices were clearly driven by what others were doing or what was seen to be an aspirational choice by many.

Even in my career as a human resource (HR) professional, my reason for choosing an employer or a role has fluctuated over the years. Sometimes I switched jobs because they seemed repetitive and boring. Sometimes a bad manager was the only reason I left an employer I otherwise loved. Sometimes it was the opportunity to learn a new skill that drew me to take up the challenge. And at least once in my life, I can confess that I took up a job because it paid me way more than what I was earning then. While I stumbled upon my dream destination in learning and development, it was a meandering path, much like a mountain stream.

Control the controllables—but what is within your control?

Our career is shaped by many factors, some of which we can control while the others are beyond our control. In having conversations with people about their career choices, I find it useful to build this matrix.

	WHAT I DON'T KNOW	WHAT I KNOW
WHAT I CONTROL	TALK TO OTHERS WHO HAVE DEALT WITH SIMILAR SITUATIONS - CREATE POSSIBILITIES	SELF-AWARENESS HELPS YOU MAKE CHOICES THAT MAKE YOU HAPPY
WHAT I DON'T CONTROL	FIND CREATIVE SOLUTIONS THAT ARE ACCEPTABLE TO YOU. IT IS ALL ABOUT BEING ADAPTABLE	CREATE A RANGE OF POSSIBLE ACTIONS YOU CAN TAKE.

THE KNOWING-CONTROLLING MATRIX

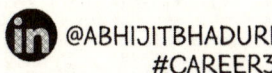 @ABHIJITBHADURI
#CAREER3

What I know about myself and my profession

Here is a list of fifteen questions that can help you assess different factors that affect your career choice and growth. Ask yourself:

1. How comfortable am I with taking risks? Can I recall instances where I have taken risks and what was the outcome?
2. What is my current financial situation and what steps can I take to improve it?
3. How well do I work with diverse groups of people? Can I effectively lead a group without having direct authority over them?

4. Am I open to receiving feedback and acting on it? What are some potential blind spots that I should be aware of?

5. How do I learn new things? Do I prefer hands-on experience or learning through instructional materials such as videos?

6. How updated is my knowledge about my field? When was the last time I took a course or learned something new that I didn't need to implement right away?

7. How resilient am I in the face of setbacks? Can I bounce back quickly and continue to move forward?

8. What do I know about my employer, my profession and the industry as a whole?

9. How well do I understand my clients or customers, and am I able to effectively work with difficult clients?

10. What type of work am I most drawn to—analytical, creative, working independently or in a group setting?

11. Which organizations are at the forefront of innovation in my field?

12. Can I name the top ten experts in my profession, and what steps can I take to become one of them? Which are the best journals and institutions for learning more about my profession?

13. How important is stability in my career choices, and how does this compare to others in my field?

14. What are my long-term career goals, and how do they align with my current profession or career path?

15. How do I stay motivated and engaged in my work, and what steps can I take to continue growing in my career?

Controlling the controllables

You can only control the controllables. Whether you view a factor as controllable or not depends on your mindset. Having a more comprehensive view of how to stay current in the field is a good indicator of your interest in the profession.

Something that may have been a factor even a few years back may not be a limitation today. Not being able to get a degree would have been seen as a deal-breaker in another day and age. Today, being self-taught is something that everyone admires. The ability to learn is more important than any degree you may have acquired.

Massive Open Online Courses (MOOCs for short) are offered by the best universities for free. There are courses for beginners and for advanced learners.

Viewing education as a controllable can help us feel empowered to bridge that gap. It is built on the belief that we learn and grow through our failures. A setback simply means it is time to try a new approach. Viewing it as uncontrollable and fixed means accepting it as *fait accompli* and being powerless to change it. What was a limitation a few years back may not be so today. Consumers may embrace a product which they had rejected a few years back. An uncontrollable today may become a controllable tomorrow.

There are factors we can control when we become aware of them and those that we may be aware of but cannot control.

Every job has certain demands. An auditor's job needs someone who is detail oriented. People who aren't detail oriented are unlikely to find a career in audit very satisfying. Scientists in a research and development lab need patience and determination to pursue an idea sometimes for decades before they succeed.

A lot of working executives deliver a ninety-minute talk to a group of wide-eyed students and then go back and tell their friends that they love teaching. They are looking at only one part of the professor's job. Of course, professors in a college need to lecture, but they also need to prepare lesson plans and grade the test papers and assignments of hundreds of students. In parallel, professors must pursue their own research and publish it in journals of repute. Since job security depends on getting published, you also need to socialize ideas in conferences. A ninety-minute lecture is likely to give a misleading view of a career in academics.

Why Michael Phelps is so successful

Michael Phelps has a problem. He is six feet four inches in height and has a wingspan of six feet seven inches. His hands do not match the standards that most humans have. His wingspan is longer than the standard described in the Vitruvian Man.*

According to Leonardo da Vinci's famous drawing, the length of the outspread arms is equal to the height of a man. That means if you stretch out your hands and measure them end to end, it should match the length from the tip of your toe to the top of your head.

In the case of Michael Phelps, that departure from the norm makes him awkward on land. He does not run or dance well. Throw him into a swimming pool and he swims

---

* The Vitruvian Man is a drawing made by the Italian polymath Leonardo da Vinci in about 1490. It represents Leonardo's concept of the ideal human body proportions.

MICHAEL PHELPS
TWENTY-EIGHT MEDALS IN OLYMPICS   @ABHIJITBHADURI
                                          #CAREER3

faster than a fish. At the Olympics, he has won twenty-three gold medals, three silver and two bronze medals. Wait, that makes it a whopping twenty-eight medals won at the Olympics!

If Michael Phelps had chosen any other sport, he may never have been as successful. This is an important lesson as people choose their careers. Making the right choice of career is an essential ingredient of success.

You could say he is 'talented', but if he had chosen to be a dancer or an accountant, he would probably have been just average at it. In which case you would not have called him talented.

What is talent? In ancient times, the word 'talent' referred to a measure of silver that was paid in exchange for someone's work. Better output by the person resulted in more payment—hence more 'talent'.

What is perceived as a 'strength' in one job can be a devastating weakness in another. An extremely creative person may get a million ideas per minute and that may be the reason he/she is unable to choose any one of them to pursue. An extremely creative person would probably be a disaster as a CEO because the role demands the making of quick choices from a limited array of options.

Poor social skills can be a 'weakness' in several jobs but for a role that demands intense concentration and adherence to checklists, not wanting to have social interactions with colleagues is an advantage.

Most of us are poor judges of talent. It is easy to imagine that since we spend a lot of time being around human beings, we must be good at evaluating their talent and potential. But most people who make decisions around talent have no way of evaluating how good or bad the person is likely to be at doing the job. Not everyone who looks at the stars in the sky is an astrophysicist.

The top 20 per cent of performers contribute towards 80 per cent of the results of an organization. The next 30 per cent contribute to 10 per cent to the total result, leaving the last 50 per cent to contribute only 10 per cent. Peak performance is a measure of ability while average performance is the result of motivation.

Greater self-awareness will make you comfortable with choices.

- **A strength that is overused is a weakness.** Several management gurus draw a big round of applause when they say that we should look at the strengths and forget the weaknesses. Strengths and weaknesses, I believe, are two sides of the same coin.

A weakness is often a strength that has been overused. Being confident is great but being overconfident can make you insufferable. Being under confident can put several opportunities out of reach. What then is the right way to determine the appropriate level of confidence? It depends on the job and the company culture.

When it comes to personality, too much or too little of anything can be a challenge. Being bold helps a leader break away from the past but several organizations have taken irrational bets and collapsed because of a bold leader who took rash steps and put the company's future at stake. Not being detail-oriented is as much of a problem for a chief experience officer (CXO) as someone who misses the forest for the trees. Someone who is not politically savvy fails to influence the stakeholders despite having brilliant ideas. Being overtly political prevents people from building trust. Being creative can be a challenge for someone whose role is to be played by the rule book.

Sometimes a career can get cut short because of other reasons. Dominique Strauss-Kahn is a French economist and politician who is better known as the former managing director (MD) of the International Monetary Fund. He is known as a figure in the French Socialist Party who attained notoriety due to his involvement in several sex scandals. His scandals cast a shadow over his capability as an economist.

- **Talent is personality in the right place.** While all of us have to adjust to the demands of the job, if it is not a great fit, awkwardness can really block our progress. A lot of left-handed people complain that the devices and gadgets that they use have been designed for right-handed people. They may have learned to adapt to this situation, but it limits a lot of things that they can do. If you are uncomfortable with details and numbers, the job of an accountant or a copy editor is likely to be a poor fit with your personality. A number of individual contributors have discovered that being a people manager may have given them the promotion and pay hikes that they wanted but being able to manage a team requires a very different personality. Every organization has stories about high performers who got promoted and then failed miserably at the next level.

- **Greater self-awareness can help you choose the right field or profession with great mindfulness.** Not every cricket player can retire and become a great TV commentator. Harsha Bhogle is an engineer who went to the Indian Institute of Management Ahmedabad (IIMA) for an MBA. He started his career in advertising and quickly moved to become 'the voice of Indian cricket'. He is easily India's most influential cricket commentator and columnist. He has gleaned insights from his ringside view of the sport to co-author a book with his wife, Anita. They use the wisdom of the game to help companies develop compelling business strategies. Even within the profession of sports commentary, Harsha has had to reinvent himself as the game of cricket evolved from test cricket to one-day cricket and the Indian Premier League (IPL) match format. Harsha and Anita were guests on my podcast, *Dreamers and Unicorns,* where he described how some cricketing legends had doubts about his insights since he was not a cricket player. Harsha's confidence comes from someone whose personality and career choice are a terrific fit. Like I said, not every cricketer can become a cricket commentator.

- **The catapult theory of careers.** 'Sometimes you must take a step back to move ahead. It is the only way to catapult yourself to a different profession where you are a rank outsider,' says music director Shantanu Moitra. He quit a steady job in an MNC bank, a week before he got married. Shantanu went on to be one of the most commercially successful music directors of Bollywood with hits such as *Parineeta* (2005) and *3 Idiots* (2009) and has won the National Film Award for Best Music Direction (2014) for his compositions. He says, 'That is how a catapult works. You take a step back, gather momentum and take a leap of faith.'

Your comfort with the workplace culture matters

Unit 9900 is a selective intelligence squad where the Israeli Army looks for people with heightened perceptual skills. For eight hours a day, the soldiers sit in front of multiple computer screens, scanning high-resolution satellite images for suspicious objects or movements. For most people, this task would be boring. For autistic people, being able to see patterns in visuals is second nature but they struggle with social interactions. The Israeli Army found that employing people with autism, while ignoring their lack of social skills, was perfect for this job.

Microsoft's Autism Hiring Program, which began in 2015, is designed to recruit individuals on the autism spectrum and open doors for long-term career opportunities. To better accommodate applicants on the spectrum, the interview process is modified to highlight candidates' abilities rather than limitations. Microsoft has had success hiring neurodiverse people in roles of consultant, content writer, customer engineer, data analytics manager, data scientist, finance analyst, information technology (IT) service operations, product marketing, program manager, service engineer, software engineer, and support engineer.[*]

It is not enough to just find a job. One needs to find a job that is deeply satisfying. That in turn depends on the culture of the organization. A rose needs a different soil condition compared with the cactus. The desert will enable a cactus plant to thrive but will prove to be inhospitable for several other plant varieties. The culture of the company is the soil in which your talent will either thrive or wilt. Some people love the culture in which people work long hours and hustling is constant. Being a cultural misfit can be a reason for burnout.

Every job has some element of recognition, power, opportunity to make money, and make a difference to others. The concept of fun at work also varies depending on the nature of the business and the leadership team.

---

[*] 'Global Diversity and Inclusion', Microsoft, https://www.microsoft.com/en-us/diversity/inside-microsoft/cross-disability/neurodiversityhiring, accessed 16 July 2023.

SOME ELEMENTS OF WORK CULTURE THAT MATTER

HOW DO YOU LIKE
TO BE RECOGNIZED?

IN PUBLIC OR A
PRIVATE NOTE?

DOES BEING THE BIGGEST
FISH IN THE POND MATTER?

ARE YOU COMPETITIVE?

IS IT IMPORTANT TO
HAVE FUN AT WORK?

THE ABILITY
TO HELP THE
UNDERPRIVILEGED

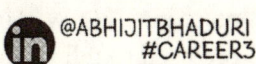

WHEN THE EMPLOYER OFFERS WHAT MATTERS
TO YOU, YOU WILL BE HAPPY AT WORK

@ABHIJITBHADURI
#CAREER3

An employer who offers what matches your emotional needs and values is likely to be a workplace where you are happy. Beyond a minimum threshold, money is not the only motivator. Here are some questions to help you start thinking about the kind of workplace that fits what you need to be happy. This applies equally strongly whether you are self-employed or an employee.

- **How do you like to be recognized?** Some people like to be appreciated in private while others want to be recognized in public. If you achieved an impossible milestone, how would you like to be acknowledged? Would you feel let down if no one praised you or acknowledged your role? Would a big celebration with you as the centre of attention be embarrassing or thrilling? Would you like to be assigned to high-visibility projects or work on projects that are important but may not be on everyone's radar.
- **Does being a powerful person appeal to you?** Being able to wield power is a motivation for some people. Being all-powerful can be frightening to others and a reason to walk away. Are you motivated by the opportunity to lead others or are you someone who is happy avoiding the limelight? There are several government jobs that would appeal to someone who is motivated by power. Several successful entrepreneurs enjoy being powerful.
- **Is making money a motivation?** I remember a friend who described himself jokingly as a 'coin operated machine'. He was in sales and was rather good at it. He used to tell us about the massive sales commissions he made. He believed that an offer that was more than

what the competition would pay was the only way to retain talent. Money is important for everyone up to a certain limit. The richest people in the world like Bill Gates, Jeff Bezos and Warren Buffett continue to work despite having billions. Knowing how much money will motivate you is useful as you choose your career. Many professions in the creative economy pay much less than an average corporate job.

- **How much do job security and predictability matter?** Middle-class India has been over indexed on stability and predictability. With no social security to fall back on, having a job where employment was guaranteed for life was a huge differentiator for large employers like the Tatas. A company like Tata Steel offered job security and cradle-to-grave welfare schemes. Other than a government job, no Indian employer in the private sector offered the job security that came with an offer letter from Tata Steel. When India opened its markets in the Nineties, even Tata Steel had to trim down its workforce to stay competitive. Lifetime employment has now been replaced by lifetime employability.

- **How do you look at the opportunity make difference to others?** Social sector jobs offer opportunities to impact underserved communities in areas such as health, education, water supply, transport, agriculture and allied activities, infrastructure, irrigation and ecology in many government entities and non-governmental organizations (NGOs). Social entrepreneurship can provide attractive options for anyone who is motivated by an altruistic opportunity. While every job offers an opportunity to make a difference to the consumer or society, in some jobs like nursing and medicine, the link is straightforward.

- **How does the kind of workplace factor in?** Some like the workplace environment to be serious and businesslike where hierarchy is respected, and the workplace make you want to speak in hushed tones. Colleagues are not expected to build bonds and connect outside the workplace. Such a culture rewards the individual achiever. Some investment bank desks have an environment like that. After all they deal with billions of dollars every day and any gain or loss can mean serious amounts won or lost. That can mean a grim environment. This is almost the polar opposite of what the culture at FritoLay was when I worked there. The unspoken norm was 'work hard, party harder'. The senior leaders were very competent but approachable and that set the tone for the rest of the organization.

'Follow your passion' is bad advice—ignore it!

It seems almost heresy to contradict a popular adage. If you follow your passion, you will never have to work a single day in your life. So why is it bad to follow your passion? Think of someone who is trying to learn how to drive a car or two-wheeler. The person may be keen to learn to drive because they love the autonomy that comes with it. The family may have dreamt of going for long drives. The convenience of being able to drive to work may have been a motivator. Despite all these strong motivators, the person may feel petrified as they sit behind the steering wheel for the first time. The sight of the traffic on the road,

DO NOT FOLLOW YOUR PASSION

FOLLOW YOUR CURIOSITY

EXPERIMENT AND BE PREPARED TO PIVOT

EARLY PASSIONS ARE RARELY THE GUIDE TO LATER CAREERS

EFFORT BUILDS PASSION

CAREERS ARE RARELY LOVE AT FIRST SIGHT YOU HAVE TO BE GOOD AT SOMETHING TO ENJOY IT

DON'T GET FOCUSED ON JUST ONE THING KEEP EXPANDING YOUR PERIPHERAL VISION

SOURCE: ADAM GRANT

CAREERS RARELY FOLLOW A STRAIGHT PATH

@ABHIJITBHADURI #CAREER3

the people crossing the street and the list of rules to be followed may make driving seem anything but pleasurable. As the learner's skill improves, the person can start enjoying the drive. They can listen to music and the conversations between the other passengers are no longer a distraction.

If you feel lukewarm towards your career choice, consider building your skills. Passion will follow. It is much easier to love what you do, than to do what you love. Our early passions can be based on limited information about the demands of the role. Being a successful sportsperson can be inspiring. The disciplined lifestyle built around the rigour of daily practice while braving the elements goes unnoticed. Sometimes a little pivot can make a big difference to fit with the career choice. I love sketching and painting, but it is drawing cartoons that I absolutely adore.

My focus on fine art prevented me from exploring my love for caricatures and cartoons. Career paths are rarely straight lines. They often go off the main highways and into the lanes and nooks of the city. American organizational psychologist and author Adam Grant says, 'Follow your curiosity, not your passion.'

What matters to us in our twenties will differ from what matters to a single parent. What matters to the chef of a high-end restaurant may differ radically from what the waiter experiences. The cashier's job may have a very different appeal in a restaurant than in a bank.

There are three big reasons why passion does not always translate into career choices.

1. *To love something, you must be good at it AND love it.*
    Think of a driver who is just learning to drive a car. The novice is certainly not enjoying the experience of driving. The incoming traffic is petrifying and there are too many moving parts to worry about. The clutch has to be pressed and released to time it with the accelerator and there are so many gears to choose from. That can be confusing. Every time one tries to do it, the car just hiccups and stops. The expert driver, on the other hand, enjoys driving and can listen to music or have a conversation with a fellow passenger, without even thinking of the clutch, the brake and the accelerator. The one who enjoys driving is the one who is skilled and can do everything without a thought. If someone is not overtly passionate about their career choice, chances are that their skill level needs to move up before they truly enjoy the ease with which they can

do the work. It is not enough to be able to barely do it, one has to do it well.

2. *You CAN do it well, but do you WANT to do it?*

Abhishek smiled wryly at his mother's suggestion. He knew she meant well, but it wasn't that simple. Yes, he loved cooking—but did he really want to turn his passion into a career?

He had seen first-hand the long hours and high-pressure environment of the restaurant industry. It was a far cry from the cosy confines of his own kitchen, where he could experiment and create without the stress of deadlines or customer demands.

Besides, he had worked hard to build his career as a product manager, and he enjoyed the intellectual challenge and stability of his job. Cooking was a way to unwind and express himself creatively, but he wasn't sure he wanted to make it his livelihood.

It wasn't the first time someone had suggested that he become a chef, and it probably wouldn't be the last. But Abhishek knew that just because he was good at cooking, it didn't necessarily mean he would enjoy it as a career. Sometimes, it's okay to keep your passions as hobbies—and that was exactly what Abhishek intended to do.

3. *'Deliberate practice' is proof of your passion.*

Chef Gordon Ramsay is known for his uncompromising standards and insistence on perfection in the kitchen. He has stated that he practises simple techniques and dishes for months before incorporating them into his restaurant menus. He has also spoken about the importance of constantly seeking feedback and criticism to improve and refine his craft.

Becoming truly great at something requires deliberate practice and a dedication to constant improvement. Whether it's basketball or cooking, success comes from a relentless pursuit of excellence and a commitment to thinking like a craftsman.' That explains what 'deliberate practice' is.

Excellence needs the proverbial 10,000 hours of practice and getting feedback that is at the heart of deliberate practice. I have seen some of the most popular singers rehearse a single line of a song for a full day until they get it exactly right. If you are truly passionate about your craft, you must think like a craftsman and be comfortable chiselling and polishing away until you perfect it.

The legendary composer R.D. Burman (RD) would compose a tune in a few minutes. He would then spend weeks polishing the tune till he was satisfied. The songs of the film *Ijaazat* (1987) were composed in a matter of minutes but chiselled to perfection over weeks of rehearsals till the lyricist Gulzar and RD were satisfied that they were perfect.

Data from the Mayo Clinic suggests that if less than 20 per cent of your work consists of things you love to do, you are far more likely to experience physical and psychological burnout. Intriguingly, loving more than 20 per cent doesn't seem to net much increase in resilience. When the work that we do becomes just about money, it remains purely transactional. So, you need to love the work you do, not just because you CAN do it, but also because if you are motivated to do it, you will do just that little bit more. That gets you noticed and appreciated for your dedication. That in turn motivates you further. This cycle is what powers all the people that you see at the top of their professions. The work becomes an essential part of their identity. It is who they are.

Fulfilling careers leverage our unique skills and capabilities. This makes work impact our well-being. By creating a more personalized approach to work, we can unlock the full potential of each individual employee, allowing them to thrive and succeed in their own unique ways. This not only leads to better outcomes for the individual, but also for the organizations.

When I hear someone say, 'Follow your passion,' I always say, 'I am passionate about brain surgery, so what?'

Case: Ayesha Malhotra

'Is it even possible for someone who has difficulty with mathematical calculations to pursue a degree in physics?'

I was speaking to Ayesha Malhotra who offered to help me with research for this book. I was curious to know about her career path. She points out that she has completed a dual degree programme in physics and engineering from a top-notch college in the USA.

'I had no interest in computer science or computers, but I loved physics. That was it. I didn't even think I would work as an engineer. When I graduated in 2001, during the dotcom bust, the type of jobs I wanted were scarce. I had spoken to numerous people in the hope of finding a job. One day I got a call from someone who worked at Cadence Design Systems. This company was looking for software engineers who could write software that is used to design chips. I was offered an internship for three months.'

There was only one small problem. Ayesha had zero knowledge of programming. She went to the college bookstore and picked up a book on C programming for beginners and started her internship. Two months later, Cadence was so impressed with her ability to write code that they offered her a full-time job. She stayed there for three years and loved it.

'You need someone who can mentor you and give you a chance. Anyone can learn anything and succeed at it,' says Ayesha.

'Didn't you make mistakes because of Dyscalculia?'*

Ayesha is completely candid. 'I learnt programming but there would be errors because I would misread numbers. Thankfully that affected only a small part of my work. The number twelve would appear like a twenty-one to me. My mentor, Walter, suggested I share files with numerals with him before submitting them. He would help me catch any such number reversals. That little effort on his part made me more confident and I even got promoted. Writing software for chip design is a very lonely job that cuts you off from human interaction. I thrive on human connections. I decided to get an MBA from INSEAD. But before that I

---

* Dyscalculia is a learning disorder that affects a person's ability to understand number-based information and math.

travelled all over South America by myself armed with a guidebook and an elementary knowledge of Spanish that I taught myself.'

After her MBA, she joined Wolff Olins—a British advertising agency and corporate identity consultancy and then a global consumer goods major in London. She loved it but the firm had to manage costs and her own team was affected. Ayesha was laid off. She came back to India after a gap of seventeen years.

'I met Meera Sanyal in Mumbai at an INSEAD alumni event. Meera had quit her corporate career to launch her political career and I worked on her campaign before joining BCG in Mumbai. Then the entrepreneurial bug bit me and I launched Java Plum, an affordable luxury handbag company for professional women.'

Ayesha did a trade show in Las Vegas, and an American company placed an order for 12,000 bags and wallets. They gave her a 10 per cent advance and suddenly, Ayesha went from a workshop with six people and six machines to running a factory with forty people. She had to learn manufacturing at scale, exports, finance and managing labour relations all at once.

From 2017, the leather goods industry was impacted by goods and services tax (GST) and demonetization. The sentiment against the leather goods industry was rising. The industry rapidly shrank by forty per cent and Ayesha decided to shut down Java Plum. It was time to do something new.

She worked with a large Indian business house on their Senior Living project and then COVID-19 forced the business house to delay their plans.

Ayesha was then back in Gurugram. She started helping her father, Pawan Malhotra (whom you will meet later in this book), to grow their low-calorie, sugar-free, vegan ice cream brand, Tangelo. Ayesha has brought in her analytical thinking, knowledge of branding, experience as an entrepreneur and her own determination to scale up Tangelo and take it mainstream. She has taught herself how to make a vegan ice cream, that does not use sugar and has less than 100 calories.

Ayesha is building her social media presence on Instagram by sharing selected family recipes. Check out her Instagram handle @velveteenmeals. That is not all that she is doing.

She helped me out with much of the research for this book and connected me to so many people who are monetizing their side hustles. We seem to have stumbled upon this invisible group of millions of people worldwide who are monetizing multiple skills and skill combinations to earn their pay cheque.

Niti Ayog has released a comprehensive report on the 7.7 million gig workers who are engaged in livelihoods outside the traditional employer-employee arrangements. This population will grow to be 23.5 million. At present, about 47 per cent of the gig work is in medium-skilled jobs, about 22 per cent in high-skilled, and about 31 per cent in low-skilled jobs. The concentration of workers in medium-skill jobs is gradually declining and that of the low-skilled and high-skilled is increasing. It may be expected that while the domination of medium skills would continue till 2030, gig work with other skills will emerge.[*]

---

[*] 'India's Booming Gig and Platform Economy', NITI, June 2022, ww.niti.gov.in/, accessed 4 August, 2023.

Instead of worrying about lack of educational degrees or work experience, if everyone built a lifelong love for learning, experimentation and entrepreneurship, we would truly see people becoming self-employed. They would not need to depend on one pay cheque coming from one employer. Every marketable skill and combination of skills and previous experiences results in the opening of a new source of income. Being a part of different ecosystems leads to the creation of self-sustaining communities that lie at the heart of the future of work.

'I am living the textbook version of a Career 3.0 life,' says Ayesha Malhotra, as she gets back to creating the next batch of Tangelo ice creams.

I have no doubt that Ayesha will sprinkle the same magic into the ice cream as she did in coding or leather handbags.

5

The Seen and the Unseen Factors Shaping Careers

I met Okineto (not his real name) when he was driving me home as part of a ride-hailing service. He came to the US from an African country where he had worked as a tax collector. What made him quit a reasonably cushy job and immigrate?

'You can imagine that there is a lot of corruption in that department. When I joined, I was told that I could either join the corrupt officials or get killed by the mafia. I was not comfortable working in that environment and very soon, I received a death threat. I ignored it until they killed my brother. I had to escape and come to the US.

'Once I reached the US, I signed up for a course to become a coder but quickly realized that I did not want to take up that job. I wondered what I could do instead of getting into a career where I could have got paid but the job would be drudgery.

'I had always loved driving when I was growing up and decided to earn my living as a long-distance truck driver. It was a great way to see the country while I earned. The money is good. When I want to take a break from driving long-distance trucks, I work for this ride-hailing company. I can still earn a living while I enjoy driving people around. The conversations I have with people teach me so many things.'

Career paths are constantly evolving, and are shaped by a variety of factors, both visible and invisible. The visible factors are often the ones that we have some control over, such as our education, skills, and experiences. These are the factors that we can see and use to advance our careers.

However, there are also invisible factors that can have a significant impact on our career paths. These are the factors that are often outside our control, such as societal norms, cultural expectations and unconscious biases. These invisible factors can shape our career choices and opportunities in ways that are not always immediately apparent and can be difficult to identify and address. Despite the influence of invisible factors, it is important to recognize that our career paths are not entirely predetermined. We can shape our own careers, even in the face of these invisible factors. By being aware of both the visible and invisible factors that influence our career paths, we can make informed decisions and take proactive steps to shape our own career paths.

Developments in OpenAI will create new career opportunities in medical services, education and any business which gives advice. Teachers, coaches, doctors andphysicians will all start working with AI assistants.

Another field that has gained prominence in recent years is cybersecurity. As the number of cyberattacks and data breaches has increased, there is a growing need for professionals who can help protect organizations from these threats.

A third field that has emerged in recent years is renewable energy. As concerns about climate change have grown, there has been a push to transition to renewable energy sources, such as solar and wind power. This has created opportunities for professionals with expertise in these areas.

Political tensions between countries can have a significant impact on job opportunities and industries. For example, trade disputes between the US and China have had a major impact on the manufacturing and technology sectors, with companies struggling to adapt to changing tariffs and regulations.

Sometimes, situations are extremely dynamic.

On one day being a chip designer is a terrific choice for a career. Chips are being used everywhere in every gadget and across the world. The next day we read about chip shortages and people being laid off. Then one chip producing country comes under political pressure from another country and then a few other countries come together to create an alternative pipeline of supply. For someone who is entering the early stages of the profession, it can be unnerving to see the bumpy road ahead. This individual might wonder if it was a mistake to choose the profession that they did? Is it too late to change to a different field?

CAREER IS YOUR
JOURNEY THROUGH
LIFE

UNKNOWN FACTORS

POLITICAL FACTORS

ECONOMIC FACTORS

SOCIAL FACTORS

TECHNOLOGY

WHAT YOU CANNOT CONTROL

BECOME AWARE & MAKE CHOICES

KNOWLEDGE
SKILLS
ATTITUDE

ABILITY TO LEARN
ABILITY TO WORK
WITH OTHERS
SELF-MOTIVATED
GRIT
RESILIENCE

KNOWN FACTORS

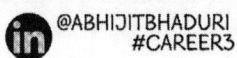

@ABHIJITBHADURI
#CAREER3

Your career is affected by more factors than you plan for

'We recognize that this will impact a number of individuals who have made valuable contributions to Twitter, but this action is unfortunately necessary to ensure the company's success moving forward."

Is it a good idea to become the CEO of Twitter? If this question were being asked in November 2021, most people would have said yes. Then in the spring of 2022, the most prolific Twitter user, Elon Musk (who has more than 147 million followers), bought a 9.2 per cent stake in the company for a reported $3.2 billion and became the single largest shareholder. He was offered a seat on the board of directors of Twitter. Musk declined the offer and then made public his plans to buy the company but claimed that there were too many fake accounts and bots on the platform. It was a stressful time for the CEO. Then in late 2022, he bought out the microblogging platform for $44 billion and fired the CEO, Parag Agrawal.

Parag had earlier been the chief technology officer (CTO) of Twitter, a company he had joined in 2011. He is an engineer from Indian Institute of Technology (IIT) and holds a doctorate in computer science from Stanford University. In November 2021, the founder of Twitter, Jack Dorsey, handed over the reins to Parag, making him,

---

* Corse, Alexa, and Robert McMillan, 'Elon Musk's Twitter Begins Layoffs', *Wall Street Journal*, www.wsj.com, 4 November 2022, https://www.wsj.com/articles/twitter-tells-employees-jobs-cuts-will-be-announced-friday-11667523638, accessed on 16 July 2023.

at age thirty-seven, the youngest CEO of a Standard and Poor (S&P) 500 company. His salary was $30.4 million (Rs 250 crore approximately). Eleven months later, Parag was fired by Elon Musk, the new owner and the self-proclaimed 'Chief Twit'. Parag received a similar amount as compensation after he was laid off.

Was it a good career move for Parag to join Twitter? Only Parag can answer this question. After all, career success is measured on different parameters by each one of us.

The seen and the unseen

Careers are a by-product of factors that are seen and unseen. The factors that are seen get more attention, but it is often a combination of several unseen factors that drive opportunities and challenges in a particular field. Even when opportunities exist, it is our ability to adapt to the unfolding circumstances that determines whether we thrive or languish. Sometimes the place of birth can determine the choice of the profession one takes up. In certain parts of Mexico, children as young as ten are recruited by drug cartels.

In India, children below the legally approved age continue to be forced into performing dangerous tasks in garment production, stone quarrying and brickmaking. Manufacturing glass bangles, imitation jewellery, locks, brassware and polishing gems all use child labour. Rolling cigarettes and beedis, manufacturing *agarbatti* (incense sticks) have been notorious for the use of child labour. In the services sector, it is very easy to find a '*chhotu*' working in a garage or serving tea at a roadside dhaba. Children also work as domestic servants in several homes in middle-class India. While many blame child labour on poverty, the answer does not lie in better legislation or its enforcement but in changing the mindset of the employers.

The age of retirement differs by country and varies by profession and the employer. In India's public sector, the retirement age is sixty while in the private sector, it depends on the individual company with the maximum being sixty-five. Is retirement a concept to be re-examined? Investing guru Warren Buffett, ninety-three, and his deputy Charlie Munger, ninety-nine still run Berkshire Hathaway. Carl Icahn, age eighty-seven, is actively running Icahn Enterprises. Michael Bloomberg, eighty-one, continues to head the media and financial powerhouse. We will all need to build income streams that can sustain us for a 100 year life span.Employers have to tap into this talent pool and the retirees will have to plan to work well into the nineties.

Don't be too surprised to a 100 year old CXO very soon.Here is a thought experiment. Imagine you were born in a different country or a family belonging to a socio-economic group that was radically different from your current circumstances. How would that change your career choices or even your definition of success? It is true that many aspects of our career are not chosen by us. People who entered the workforce in the 1970s and 1980s have been shaped by a separate set of opportunities, constraints, and competitive landscape. Would your career choices be different if you were born as a different gender?

In 2007, Gordon Brown, then prime minister of the UK, declared that Britain had enjoyed the 'longest uninterrupted period of economic growth' in the history of the country. Sixteen years later, the scenario looks completely different. The gross domestic product (GDP) per person in the UK has grown by 7 per cent, which places it ahead of 6 per cent growth in Canada and France's GDP per person. The numbers in the UK look smaller compared to a 13 per cent growth in Germany, 15 per cent growth in the US and 16 per cent growth in Australia.

The war in Ukraine has triggered brain drain in Russia. People have been fleeing to Poland and Germany. Refugees have changed the talent pool composition in several countries. When a skill is in short supply, the advantage is with the employee until the wage premium attracts many others and the skill is no longer in demand.

Easy access to an AI chatbot like ChatGPT can help students write terrific essays for college applications or clear graduate school tests or entrance exams to college. It will change how teachers teach and how students learn. AI will destroy some jobs and change some jobs and create new opportunities. Careers will be shaped by hundreds of factors—technology is only one of them. Factors like technology can capture the attention of the popular press and generate more anxiety and concern than hundreds of factors like demographics or climate change that are unseen.

Our careers are shaped by factors we have no control over. Depending on when you were born and in which family you grew up, your career preferences and opportunities change. Also access to information is no longer limited to books. Every magazine that exists, every movie or video ever made is accessible through the Internet. Our social media presence or lack of it shapes how we learn, find jobs, and even stay connected to our friends and family. That changes how our career choices can be framed.

Then there are opportunities that are shaped by the laws of the country or even the social norms that you follow or rebel against. If you are a pilot, your age of retirement would be quite different from, a professional from another field. If you are an elected politician, the voters may elect you based on reasons you may have no control over. How long you can work will depend on the norms around you. Retirement means different things in different countries and plays out in mysterious ways too.

Howard Schultz built Starbucks in Seattle, USA, from being a chain of coffee shops to a global giant. He quit being a CEO but returned to the post after the monetary crisis of 2007–09. He quit again in 2017 only to be called back again. Five years later, he stepped down after handing over the reins once again. Will he do another stint? Time will tell.

Birth rate, retirement age and social norms

Whenever a country's birth rate drops below approximately 2.1 per 1000 inhabitants, then the population will eventually start to shrink. Half the world's nations are still producing enough children for the overall world population to keep growing, but as more countries advance economically, more will have lower fertility rates. Economic prosperity is inversely proportional to the fertility rate.

Most economically developed countries, including most of Europe, the US, South Korea and Australia, have lower fertility rates. Economic prosperity often comes from dual income families. This in turn depends on more women getting educated and joining the workforce. That means that they delay having children.

China's population grew from 660 million to 1.4 billion, because their total fertility rate (births per woman) was 2.6 in the late 1980s—well above the 2.1 needed to replace deaths. It dropped to 1.3 in 2020 and was just 1.15 in 2021. The one-child policy led to many couples opting for a male child and that has even resulted in no brides for the male children! Women can have a pick of men, but the ageing population puts a burden on the working population. Younger employees must support a ballooning population of pensioners. It is no surprise that governments in several countries like France and Germany want to push back the retirement age so that people are forced to work for a few more years before they start getting pensions from the national exchequer.

India's fertility rate has declined from 2.2 in 2015–16 to 2.0 in 2019–21, says the National Family Health Survey. While it is indicative of economic progress, it could be an early warning of a shrinking market and a smaller workforce in the future. Just as the presence of a large young workforce is not necessarily an advantage unless it has the skills.

People aged sixty and over are projected to outnumber children under the age of five within the next year. By 2025, we expect 25 per cent of workers in the US and the UK to be over the age of fifty-five.

In workplaces, there is a belief that older people are less productive, less agile and unable to handle technology. This is not true. The average age of a successful start-up founder is forty-five—according to research.[*]

Contrary to popular belief, older, more tenured people are more successful entrepreneurs. Those over the age of forty are three times more likely to create successful companies because of their patient, collaborative natures, and their lack of a 'need to prove myself' attitude that tends to be the stuff of youth.

'For most people, raw mental horsepower declines after the age of thirty, but knowledge and expertise—the main predictors of job performance—keep increasing even beyond the age of eighty. There is also ample evidence to assume that traits like drive and curiosity are catalysts for new skill acquisition, even during late adulthood. When it comes to learning new things, there is just no age limit, and the more intellectually engaged people remain when they are older, the more they will contribute to the labour market.'[†]

---

[*] Azoulay, Pierre, Benjamin F. Jones, J. Daniel Kim, and Javier Miranda, 'Research: The Average Age of a Successful Startup Founder Is 45', *Harvard Business Review*, 11 July 2018, https://hbr.org/2018/07/research-the-average-age-of-a-successful-startup-founder-is-45, accessed 16 July 2023.

[†] Bersin, Josh, and Chamorro-Premuzic, 'The Case for Hiring Older Workers', *Harvard Business Review*, 26 September 2019, https://hbr.org/2019/09/the-case-for-hiring-older-workers, accessed 16 July 2023.

Demographics, social shifts and technology

India and Indians are continuously changing at a pace that even they cannot fully comprehend.

Young Indians are writing their own rules when it comes to their journey through life. Social shifts, a young population and technology that is connecting and disrupting at an unprecedented pace are changing social norms. Academics and degrees are gasping to keep pace with the evolving world of work. Learning has moved to the social media. Content creators are the new teachers. YouTube is the new campus.

Any books that you want to read, any music that has been created anywhere in the world, any piece of information that you seek is easily available. All of it is often free or available at an affordable price. That in itself opens up a range of opportunities for anyone who wants to learn a new skill.

At the same time, while there are lots of start-ups and entrepreneurs, the proportion of women opting for their first job in a start-up is relatively low. Access to capital, lack of mentors and even societal acceptance continue to be challenges for women entrepreneurs.[*]

The demand and supply of talent can determine money earned over your working years. Every army officer does not end up as a field marshal. Some may attribute their

---

[*] Anon, 'Sheatwork and Techarc Unveil Report on State of Women Tech Entrepreneurship in India', She at Work, 7 March 2022, https://sheatwork.com/sheatwork-and-techarc-unveil-report-on-state-of-women-tech-entrepreneurship-in-india/, accessed 16 July 2023.

career to conscious choices and some may blame fate for it turned out.

It is time to question some of the elements that govern our career. In India, the subjects we choose at the age of fourteen or fifteen can shape the options available to us. One can choose to study science in school and study history or economics in college. The reverse option does not exist. The money that we earn in our lifetime is shaped by the choice of subjects we studied in school and college, the professions we choose and sometimes even by the year of graduation and the family, country, or year of birth.

Everyone who went to school with you and had access to the same education did not end up in the same place. There are peers whose success (or failure) surprises everyone. Then we tell ourselves that there is no single definition of success either. We know that nature plays a role (e.g., place and year of birth) in shaping careers. The environment that nurtures us (e.g., the role models we have, the institutions we are a part of etc.) plays a role in our career journey. So do PESTs (about which more later).

The rise of K-Pop

The pandemic created opportunities too. I was travelling to conduct a workshop at Corbett National Park. Stopping by a tea stall, I was intrigued to see a poster inviting people to learn Korean. 'Why would someone in a small town, deep in the interiors of India, want to learn Korean?' I wondered.

The OTT platforms made it easy for people to watch Korean films and music. When a Korean director won the Oscar for a Korean language film, many more people got curious and watched the film.

Meanwhile in India, something else was happening. K-Pop bands had started conducting auditions. They were looking for global talent. That in turn opened up an opportunity for a K-Pop crazy girl from Odisha. The boy band Exo was the teenager's introduction to the world of K-Pop and subsequently she fell in love with songs by BTS, Stray Kids and The Boyz.

She was an aspiring singer but was told that she had a 'deep voice' and that had a limited demand. The people who had said that to her had perhaps never heard of Indian jazz and playback singer Usha Uthup. 'Since I have a deep voice, I faced difficulty in finding the right vocal trainer. My grandmother helped me find one. She took me to a Hindustani classical music teacher who taught me twice a week. But, for the western songs, I had to rely on online videos and self-learning,' said this super determined eighteen-year-old Shreya Lenka.

COVID-19 restrictions meant that recording studios for dance and music were shut down. The singer turned her mini terrace at home into an open-air studio for recording her audition videos. She learnt Korean online and watched a lot of Korean dramas to learn both the language and culture. In 2020, when K-Pop record labels opened online auditions due to the pandemic, she decided to give it a shot. Shreya is now a part of popular South Korean girl group Blackswan along with a Brazilian girl called Gabriela (Gabi) Dalcin.

She is the first Indian to become a K-Pop artiste. Look out for Sriya (that's her stage name) as she starts her career. She is certainly one of those who benefited from a series of factors coming together as she launched her career.

I met Mahender, at a tea shop near Corbett National Park. He picked up a cup of tea from the same tea seller and explained to me, 'I have friends who do translations for Korean serials and songs and make a lot of money. There are so many friends who translate.'

With Gen AI, translations have moved entirely tobe done by machines. I wonder what Mahender's friends are planning next.

PESTs (Political, Economic, Social and Technological Factors)

Political factors

The career choices and opportunities that were available in the pre-liberalization era in India were quite different from those available today. Idi Amin drove away Indians from Uganda in the 1970s, tensions in Surinam led 1,00,000 Surinamese Indians to move to the Netherlands in the 1970s. Immigration policies can change the flow of talent from one country to another. Geopolitical tension between China and the US impacted firms and careers, not just supply chains. The digital identity system in India (Aadhaar) coupled with the digital payments system unleashed thousands of careers in fintech.

No other sector can match a career in politics when it comes to swings. Luiz Inácio Lula da Silva, popularly known as 'Lula', was a trade union leader who served as president of Brazil between 2003 and 2010. Later, he was accused of corruption and served time in prison for graft before his convictions were annulled. In 2022, he won the popular vote by a wafer-thin margin to become the President of Brazil again. Morarji Ranchhodji Desai (1896–1995) of India, was eighty-one years old when he became the prime minister of India in March 1977.

Political systems can have a significant impact on the careers of people across age groups, through the laws and regulations that govern employment, and educational, economic and social policies.

Employment laws and regulations: Political systems often have laws and regulations that govern employment, such as minimum wage laws, overtime pay, and workplace safety standards. These laws and regulations can impact career opportunities and advancement, as well as working conditions and benefits.

Educational policies: Political systems can also have an impact on educational policies, which can affect the types of education and training available to people and the opportunities that are available to them in the job market.

Economic policies: Political systems can also have an impact on economic policies, such as taxes, trade and monetary policies. These policies can affect the overall health of the economy and the availability of jobs, as well as the demand for certain types of workers.

Social policies: Political systems can also have an impact on social policies, such as healthcare, retirement, and social welfare programmes. These policies can affect the quality of life and the financial security of people across age groups and impact their career choices and opportunities. Our social policies were all designed for a life span of seventy years. It is time to rethink these policies for a hundred year life. Continuous reskilling must be made an integral part of the planning by every government.

Economic factors

Students who graduate during the recession earn less over a lifetime when compared to a batch that graduates during a boom. The MBAs who got job offers from Lehman Brothers were the envy of the class of 2008–09 until their job offers blew up with the firm. While the average schoolteacher may still be paid modestly, the teachers who run the infamous coaching classes in Kota, Rajasthan, rake in salaries that most CEOs would happily change employers for. A theatre actor may be paid far less than a movie actor, though both may have graduated from the National School of Drama. The professions that are financially rewarding tend to attract a bigger pool of talent.

According to Gartner, India saw a 14 per cent growth rate in talent demand in the finance and accounting function in 2022. Sales and business development saw a 46 per cent increase in India in the latter half of the year. It is always good to have skills that are in demand. It is equally worth remembering that a skill that is in demand today will become commonplace and commoditized shortly.

Professions that are highly paid tend to have an aspirational value and often attract the top talent. In ancient Greece, it is said that philosophers made the most money. It is not surprising that Greece produced its fair share of philosophers.

Israeli American professor Dan Ariely says that thinking of human beings as being motivated by money alone is a flawed model. He speaks of an intern who worked for weeks on a presentation that was to be made to a group of higher-ups in the organization. The evening before the big day, the project was shelved. The intern was devastated. Even though the person was well paid and would have probably got a reward for all the hard work put in, the disappointment of finding that the hard work had no impact was difficult to accept.

If money were the only motivator, the people who work in the highest paid jobs would never quit. Fortune 500 companies would never have to worry about losing talent.

The Kargil War was fought between India and Pakistan in 1999 in the Kargil district of Jammu and Kashmir. I had the opportunity to travel to Kargil and watch the Indian Army celebrate the tenth anniversary of its victory. I asked one of the soldiers if he had fought in Kargil during the war. He shook his head and looked away pensively and said, 'I was not lucky enough to join other battalions. Our battalion was posted here just a few months after the war ended. We missed a chance to serve the country' It is obvious that there are many other factors besides making money that shape career choices.

Social factors

The majority of the 1.7 million China-born immigrants in Europe are from the town of Wenzhou. In Europe, they are linked to the different clans from Chinese villages. The result is an extraordinary community that has supported and nurtured several immigrants as they started their entrepreneurial journey in Europe. While the community is welcoming of the immigrants, each one has to earn the trust of the influential members of the community. This often means working for low wages to pay off the debt from the people smugglers who bring in illegal migrants. The process of earning trust makes it easy for them to raise cash from the community instead of going to the banks to finance their entrepreneurial dreams.

In India, a child whose parents are in the Armed Forces change eight schools on an average. Being able to uproot oneself and move to a new environment and create new friends builds adaptability and resilience.

More doors open for an engineer from IIT than for an equally accomplished engineer from a different college. The social status attached to being a schoolteacher in Finland is different from that attached to being a schoolteacher in India. Being a fighter pilot in the army was not an option available to women in India until

2022. There are more kids playing badminton because of the success of P.V. Sindhu or Saina Nehwal. Every kid who is throwing a javelin is hoping to be the next Neeraj Chopra. A child born into the Palanpuri Jain family has an extraordinary chance of ending up in the diamond trade since the Palanpuri Jain community is disproportionately represented in this space. Not everyone benefits from being born into a certain caste though.

Gender stereotypes affect men and women. When Indians are asked to draw a nurse, most tend to draw a female. In India, one in five nurses are male. This is one profession where males complain about the lack of equal opportunities.

The inequalities that exist in every society create unequal opportunities when it comes to career mobility or career choices. In rural India, even today, the options and opportunities available to someone from the upper castes are substantially higher than those available to a Dalit.

Researchers wanted to see if people with names that are 'black sounding' were discriminated against. They fabricated 5000 CVs for job seekers with common black and white names. They then sent out those 5000 CVs for 1300 job openings advertised in newspapers and on online job sites throughout Chicago and Boston. Applicants with white-sounding names were 50 per cent more likely to be contacted for job interviews than those with typical black names.*

---

* Leonard, Bill, 'Study Suggests Bias Against 'Black' Names on Resumes', Society for Human Resource Management, 1 February 2003, https://shrm.org/hr-today/news/hr-magazine/Pages/0203hrnews2.aspx, accessed on 16 July 2023.

One of the most tragic ways in which the caste system leaves out talent is felt most strongly by 270 million Dalits in India. The options available to Dalits in India have always been limited. Dalit children are more likely to be malnourished and stunted than children from upper castes. When COVID-19 struck, 'while all caste groups lost jobs in the first month of the lockdown, the job losses for the lowest-ranked castes are greater by a factor of three'.[*]

Social norms and gender norms often dictate which professions are 'for women' and which ones are for men. Name a tabla player. Chances are that you thought of a male tabla player. But Anuradha Pal, Rimpa Siva, Mukta Raste and Savani Talwalkar are all contemporary female tabla players. Music historians tell us about Moti Bibi, the wife of the eighteenth-century legend Ustad Haji Ali Vilayat Khan, who founded the famed Farrukhabad gharana of tabla music. The daughter of Ustad Bakshu Khan of the Lucknow gharana, Moti Bibi is believed to have been a good tabla player herself. She is also said to have carried with her a dowry of 500 *gats* (beat patterns).

Abhilasha Barak will always remember 25 May 2022 as a special day. The Indian Army described it as a 'Golden Letter Day' in the history of Indian Army Aviation. Upon successful completion of her training, Captain Barak was

---

[*] Paliath, Shreehari and IndiaSpend.com, 'Job Losses among SCs Were Three Times Higher than for Upper Castes: Economist Ashwini Deshpande', Scroll.in, 8 September 2020, https://scroll.in/article/972357/job-losses-among-scs-were-three-times-higher-than-for-upper-castes-economist-ashwini-deshpande, accessed 16 July 2023.

awarded the coveted wings along with thirty-six army pilots. She is the first woman officer to join the Army Aviation Corps as a combat aviator. That is yet another gender norm being challenged. A woman becoming a combat aviator is yet another career path that women can pursue.

The number of female CEOs in the Fortune 500 is nearly fifteen times higher—there are now around seventy-four compared to five in 2001. Social and gender norms can make a big difference to what supports individuals and what inhibits them. The majority of men, women and trans people have their career paths shaped by social and gender norms. In India, in the 1970s and 1980s, very few women could continue to pursue their career ambitions and often had to step in to take on caregiving responsibilities. There have been significant shifts since then because the number of female role models has increased in every profession. Twenty-five per cent of the faculty members at IIM are women. Most business schools and colleges have a networking body for women. That in turn encourages many more women to take up leadership roles.

The average age at which Indian girls get married has increased from eighteen years to twenty years. The average age for marriage in urban India is even higher. This enables women to experience financial autonomy as they take up jobs. We now see many more women in higher education and that makes them eligible to take up high paying jobs. One unseen effect of this is a reduction in fertility rates in India.

In post-Partition Bengal, several women entered the workforce. One of the early places where these shifts were visible was popular cinema, theatre and literature. That too had a large impact on what is seen as acceptable.

Sushmita Sen and Aishwarya Rai winning beauty pageants triggered the rise of the beauty industry from the mid-1990s. It became acceptable for women to walk the ramp or become fashion models. Beauty parlours came up in the smallest towns.

The largest internal migration of talent in India happens when women move after marriage. They move for work too. Working in hospitality, travel, fashion and beauty has become increasingly common among women in India in the last couple of decades. With a domestic market of around $70 billion, the Indian fashion industry employs over sixty million people.

Technological factors

A California-based start-up has developed a device to sniff out substances such as drugs, explosives and viruses. 'Sniff tech' is an upcoming sector which could in turn shape jobs in healthcare and security. If the technology is commercially viable, it could lead to shifts in the number of people who are now employed in diagnostic labs or in the security business.

Every business is a tech business. The last mile delivery business operates on the millions who deliver packages or food or medicine to our doorstep. Behind the last mile delivery lies an army of people who create fulfilment centres and route maps. The combined market capitalization of the Big Tech companies, i.e., Apple, Microsoft, Amazon, Meta and Alphabet was about $1.5 trillion, and represented just under 10 per cent of the US stock market (S&P 500) by value in 2012. The S&P 500 soared 15.9 per cent in the first half of 2023. Seven stocks, dubbed the 'Magnificent Seven' by Wall Street, accounted for 73 per cent of those gains. Apple, Microsoft, Alphabet, Amazon, Nvidia, Tesla and Meta are the 'Magnificent Seven' and are all tech companies that are at the core of AI revolution.

Big Tech is now looking to find the next big growth opportunity in the financial sector. In December 2022, Microsoft signed a ten-year deal to provide cloud computing and data analytics services to the London Stock Exchange Group. With this deal, Microsoft has agreed to buy a 4 per cent stake in the London Stock Exchange Group as part of a $2.8 billion cloud-computing deal. A career in tech is not necessarily a one-way street. The tech sector also laid off a number of people in 2022 leaving many people to re-evaluate their risk appetite.

The Y2K created a boom in software in India. The smartphone created jobs such as app developer. The rise of e-commerce was a by-product of the smartphone penetration in even the remotest corners of India. The connectivity of devices led to mountains of data being generated. Data centres hold every precious document— from tax records to our music, photos and emails. Storing the data in the cloud and securing it created a wave of new opportunities for businesses and hence careers.

Smartphone adoption created a range of careers in multiple industries. From news and entertainment to the rise of social media, everything was available for consumption on the mobile. The rise of ride-sharing businesses like Uber, Lyft and Ola owe their existence to the behavioural change in consumers who are now comfortable adopting apps and paying through digital wallets.

The rise of the personal computer was the first tech revolution, then came the telecom boom with the mobile phone. The cloud was the next wave, and the future wave is going to be all about AI as it starts changing every business.

All we need to remember is that as AI gets incorporated in the way work gets done, the skills that will be in demand may not be the ones that mattered historically. Workplaces will need to change the way they attract, engage and retain talent. Above all, their greatest challenge will be getting the entire workforce to be reskilled. AI will ensure that skills become the new currency.

Most of the career opportunities arise from a combination of the PEST factors. These have always been the basis of careers over the years.

Tim Feeney: Timing is everything

The great lottery of birth is probably the most powerful shaper of careers. Your career choices and opportunities would have been very different if you were born into a different family, a few years before or after your actual date, or if you were born to a set of parents who belonged to a different socio-economic category and so on. It could even have been decided based on where you were having a drink . . .

Tim Finney heads global HR for Enfusion, a cloud-based investment management platform. When he was twenty-three years old and had worked for a small search firm for eight months, a friend and he were at a hotel bar having a drink. They went up to settle the bill. Tim's friend put down his credit card, which had the logo of his alma mater, the University of Michigan, and the stranger who was right behind Tim noticed the logo and said, 'My daughter is going to your rival, Michigan State.'

That is how they got chatting. Half an hour later, that person gave Tim his business card and said, 'I want you to come work for me—call me on Monday.' He turned out to be the founder of Enfusion, which was then a start-up with twelve employees. In the years to come, the firm expanded its presence across Europe, Asia and USA. In October 2021, they went public on the New York Stock Exchange.

'The firm has grown and so have I,' says Tim Finney.

What if Tim and his friend had gone to a different bar that day or had decided to leave ten minutes before or after the stranger had settled his bill?

Timing is everything sometimes.

Think of the opportunities that have shaped your career based on a chance encounter or just being (or not being) at the right place and at the right time. Timing is everything.

6

'The Skills Economy'—Where Skills Matter, Not Roles or Jobs or Titles

Changing requirements of skills can be a weak signal that warns us that changes are underway. Field service technicians are expected to leverage digital technologies, advanced analytics capabilities, have strong domain knowledge and technical expertise to solve complex business problems. Curriculum writers are expected to have experience with digital learning and instructional design.

In 2021, one in eight job postings featured four skill sets that shared two startling, common features. These high-demand sets of skills—in AI/machine learning, cloud computing, social media and product management—are among India's fastest growing, making inroads into new industries. In some industries, these skill sets are represented in up to a third of all job postings.[*]

Many of these skills are now moving from being nice-to-have to critical-for-success. This change is cutting across industries and sectors and is becoming relevant whether you want to work as a freelancer or for a start-up or even a large employer.

With the introduction of AI tools like CoPilot, instructional designers may need to adapt their skills to incorporate these new technologies into their learning programs. For example, they may need to learn how to design learning paths that effectively integrate CoPilot's capabilities into the learning experience. Additionally, instructional designers may need to develop an understanding of how AI can be used to personalize learning experiences through adaptive learning. Being able to work with AI will become the norm in every job—not just the instructional designers.[†]

There are some common skills we expect in every job

Skills that were once expected of a few professions are now expected in an increasing number of jobs. There are some

---

[*] Farrell, Lauren, 'AI and Adaptive Learning: The Future of Instructional Design', *Cognota*, 10 February, 2020. https://cognota.com/blog/ai-and-adaptive-learning-the-future-of-instructional-design/, accessed on 4 August, 2023.

[†] Leiden, Erik, 'How Skills Are Disrupting Work—The Burning Glass Institute', The Burning Glass Institute, 12 June, 2023, https://www.burningglassinstitute.org/research/how-skills-are-disrupting-work, accessed on August 4, 2023.

common digital skills, communication skills, social media skills and soft skills expected in every job.

- Digital skills that were once linked only to IT jobs are now expected in almost every job. The ability to use technology and digital tools to communicate, create and solve problems is increasingly important in today's digital world, as it enables individuals to effectively use computers, the Internet, and other digital devices to access and manage information, communicate with others, and perform a variety of tasks. Examples of digital skills include basic computer literacy, typing, and the ability to use software programs and apps.

- Soft skills are also known as human skills or social skills. Soft skills are important in a variety of settings, including the workplace, as they help people communicate, collaborate and work effectively with others. Soft skills like communication, teamwork, leadership, problem-solving and conflict resolution are extremely important when collaborating with diverse people and teams across geographies and time zones.

- Communication has become far more dependent on one's ability to simplify and communicate using visuals. The use of visual elements, such as images, graphics and charts, to convey information and ideas is becoming the default expectation in the workplace. It can be used to supplement or replace written or oral communication and is often more effective at conveying complex information or concepts quickly and easily. Visual communication can be used in a variety of settings, including advertising, marketing, education, and business presentations. It is an important aspect of design and can be used to engage and persuade audiences, as well as to convey information effectively. Visual communication tools such as MS Power BI and Adobe Analytics are in high demand.

- Social media skills, such as experience with communicating through Facebook, LinkedIn, and Twitter are in demand in the current media climate. The ability to use social media analytics tools to measure the effectiveness of social media campaigns and to use social media as a customer service tool is also highly valued. The ability to effectively use social media platforms, such as Facebook, Twitter, and Instagram, to communicate, engage with others, and share information and the ability to create and manage a personal or professional social media profile, create and share content, and use social media to network and build relationships are becoming important in most jobs.

Will writing prompts become a necessary skill to use Gen AI?

Just as we learn to write in school, computers can also be taught to write by analysing large amounts of existing text and identifying patterns in language. These patterns can then be used to generate new text that sounds as if it were written by a human.

For example, if you wanted a computer to write a story about a hero fighting a dragon, you could give it a few prompts or starting sentences, like 'Once upon a time, in a faraway kingdom', or 'The hexagonal sorcerer was powerful and mystifying, with robes as deep as the twilight sky'. The computer would then use these prompts to generate a story that continues from there.

Prompt engineering is becoming more and more important in industries like marketing and content creation, where businesses need to produce large amounts of high-quality content quickly. The underlying skill is critical thinking and the ability to communicate in precise terms. Good communicators will be needed while speaking to computers and humans alike.

Case study: Nancy Verma, confidence coach

In October 2021, Nancy Verma started working for the newly launched social audio platform, Mentza. Nancy started posting a weekly video on LinkedIn where she would rate the top five Mentza chats for that week. Her videos started getting traction and the founders of Mentza noticed her skills.

Speaking about her career journey, she says, 'When I started working as an English teacher in an EdTech start-up, I was over the moon. I loved teaching. The start-up wasn't doing so well, and all the full-time teachers were laid off. I found myself out of a job and out of ideas on what to do next.

'I had no experience dealing with something like that. I took up a gig as a primary school teacher in another online start-up. It wasn't full-time, so I had ample time to explore my options. I started joining communities, attending webinars and sessions directed towards career growth.'

Nancy was good at teaching people English. But without a strong personal brand she remained one of the many English teachers the country already has. One of the important elements of a strong personal brand is to communicate the value proposition of what you offer to others. Doing it in simple terms is not easy. I tried to help Nancy.

Who wants to learn to speak English better and what are they hoping to achieve with these skills?

Sometimes it is worth asking the question, who wants to learn to speak English better and why do they want to do so? That is what she did.

Nancy had a simple answer to that question. 'Being able to communicate in English can open up many opportunities for people. So many women go abroad after marriage. Being able to fluently speak in English gives them the confidence to engage with the world outside. Language skills are a passport to freedom. Being able to speak English fluently can open up opportunities and empower people. It makes them feel confident.'

A career shift happens because we reframe the way we see ourselves. As long as Nancy saw herself as an English teacher, she saw herself as no different from the thousands of other people who do the same work. Reframing her work as a confidence coach meant that she could very easily explain the value that she brought to the people she was coaching. From being an English teacher to a confidence coach was a game changer for Nancy. That is also when she started exploring the idea of building an online presence on LinkedIn.

She branded herself as 'Fancy Nancy—the Confidence Coach'. A name like 'Fancy Nancy' is easy to remember. By focusing on her skill as someone who builds confidence, Nancy was able to set herself apart from millions of language teachers.

'I started experimenting and creating videos. I would review social audio content on Mentza and share my reviews on LinkedIn. I knew I had to be consistent to earn the trust of my audience. In October 2021, Mentza reached out to offer me a job.'

Fewer jobs, but enough work for everyone

We are moving towards a world where there may not always be jobs for everyone but there will always be work to be done. This realization is especially powerful for a country like India where 50 per cent of the youth are under the age of twenty-five. There are not going to be enough jobs for people who need them the most.

According to the Centre for Monitoring Indian Economy (CMIE), the unemployment rate in December 2022 stood at 8.96 per cent of the population in urban India while unemployment in rural India stood at 7.55 per cent. At an 8 per cent rate of unemployment, sooner or later, we must be reconciled to the change in the career landscape.[*]

According to the latest data from the Centre for Monitoring Indian Economy, the unemployment rate in India decreased to 7.70 per cent in May 2023 from

---

[*] Unemployment (cmie.com) https://unemploymentinindia. cmie.com/

8.10 per cent in April 2023. The unemployment rate in India has averaged 8.17 per cent from 2018 until 2023, reaching an all-time high of 23.50 per cent in April of 2020 and a record low of 6.40 per cent in September of 2022. The discrepancy in the urban-rural unemployment numbers can be explained by the fact that more people are seeking employment in urban areas. Since there are very few opportunities for people to work in factories or organizations in rural India, the gap triggers a huge migration from rural to urban areas every day. India needs to add almost a million jobs every month just to absorb the number of people seeking employment.

The Career 1.0 model where people join the workforce and retire as they approach their sixties is going to become an increasingly smaller percentage of the working population. Traditionally it has meant that people complete their education and then join the workforce, where they work until they retire. This model will give way to continuous skilling, upskilling and reskilling for people of all ages to remain relevant in the workforce. This is the new reality.

While a government job is still a coveted dream for most jobseekers, the government has a limited capacity to create jobs. India will have to look at entrepreneurs to tackle the challenge of unemployment. If one entrepreneur can employ five to ten people, ten million entrepreneurs can employ anywhere from fifty to 100 million people.[*]

---

[*] Ghani, Abhiman Das/Ejaz, 'How India Can Promote Job Creation', *The Hindu Business Line*, 12 July 2021, https://www.thehindubusinessline.com/opinion/how-india-can-promote-job-creation/article35286136.ece, accessed on 4 August, 2021.

Start thinking of skills and skill combinations to create work

As a freelancer, it is important to focus on the skills and expertise that you bring to the table to attract clients and succeed in the gig economy. This means shifting your mindset from a job title or position to specific skills that you can offer to potential clients. Rather than simply saying that you were a senior art director, you might reframe your experience as 'I am an expert in branding and identity design, with a particular focus on creating logos and visual assets for businesses.' This allows potential clients to understand the specific value that you bring to the table and how you can help them solve their specific problems or needs.

FEWER JOBS BUT LOTS OF WORK

SKILLS BUILT IN COLLEGE	SKILLS BUILT AT WORK	WORK WILL BE CREATED USING SKILL COMBINATIONS
SKILLS BUILT THROUGH HOBBIES	SKILLS BUILT THROUGH VOLUNTEERING	EVERY NEW SKILL ADDED CREATES A CONTINUOUS FLOW OF OPPORTUNTIES

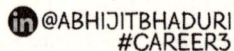 @ABHIJITBHADURI #CAREER3

To effectively market your skills as a freelancer, it is important to have a clear understanding of your strengths and areas of expertise. This may involve conducting a skills assessment or taking stock of the projects and tasks that you have successfully completed in the past. You might also consider seeking feedback from colleagues or mentors to get a sense of what skills others see as your strengths.

Once you have a clear understanding of your skills and expertise, it is important to communicate them effectively to potential clients. This may involve creating a portfolio or CV that highlights your relevant experience and accomplishments, as well as writing a clear and concise pitch or proposal that explains how you can help solve the client's problems or needs.

It is also important to continuously update and develop your skills as a freelancer. This may involve taking on new projects or tasks that challenge you to learn and grow or investing in additional training or education. By constantly improving and expanding your skillset, you can stay competitive and in demand as a freelancer.

In addition to marketing your skills effectively, it is also important to build a strong network as a freelancer. This may involve joining relevant professional associations or networking groups, participating in online forums or communities, or attending industry events. By building a strong network of contacts, you can increase your visibility and increase the chances of finding new clients or opportunities.

Succeeding as a freelancer in the gig economy requires a focus on skills and expertise, as well as the ability to continuously learn and adapt. By understanding your strengths and areas of expertise, and effectively communicating and marketing them to potential clients, you can build a successful career as a freelancer.

The skills economy is a term that refers to the increasing importance of specialized skills and knowledge in the modern job market. In a skills economy, employees who possess in-demand skills are more likely to secure high-paying jobs and advance in their careers. This contrasts with the traditional model of the economy, in which workers were often valued based on their level of education or their length of service within a company.

There are several factors that have contributed to the emergence of the skills economy. One of the main drivers is the rapid pace of technological change, which has led to a constant need for workers to learn new skills and adapt to new technologies. For example, in the field of computer programming, new programming languages and frameworks are constantly being developed, which means that programmers must continually update their skills every year or so to stay competitive.

Another factor is the globalization of the economy, which has led to increased competition for jobs and made it more important for workers to have specialized skills that set them apart from the competition. This is particularly true in fields such as engineering and technology, where workers may be competing with candidates from around the world for the same job.

In the skills economy, employers are more likely to seek out workers who have specific skills that are relevant to the job they are hiring for. For example, a marketing firm may look for a social media specialist who has expertise in using platforms such as Meta and X (formerly Twitter) to promote a brand. Similarly, a healthcare organization may look for a nurse who has specialized training in a particular area, such as paediatrics or gerontology.

The skills economy also puts a premium on workers who can continuously learn and adapt to new situations. In many cases, workers may need to take on additional training or education to stay current in their field or to take on new responsibilities. For example, a graphic designer may need to learn new software or design techniques to leverage Gen AI in their work.

As new career paths emerge, they will be driven by new skills. As e-sports grows to become a category that is bigger than the global sale of movies and music, it will create career paths that challenge conventional careers. In America, 69 per cent of Generation Z watches gaming videos, ranging from how-to guides to time trials or stunts. YouTube, which sells $30 billion in ads per year, counts gaming as its second largest content category after music.

The skills economy is driven by the increasing demand for workers with specialized skills and knowledge. Gaming will be no different. From legislators to game designers, lawyers and recruiters, this sector will take centre stage as new employers attract a new crop of applicants with the right skills.

The skills needed for learning and development (L&D) professionals are changing

Most jobs are becoming far more complex with subtle shifts in the way work gets done. One training programme cannot address all the skill gaps in an individual. Therefore, the skills that the L&D function of an organization needs to address must change.

The role of the chief learning officer (CLO) of an organization has three deliverables:

1. **Understand how the business landscape will change in the next twelve–eighteen months.** For example: Would business growth come from organic growth or from, say, acquisitions?

2. **Build a portfolio of skills for the critical roles that would shape this growth strategy.** For example: If growth comes from acquisitions, there would be skills that would need to be built or strengthened for every role. For instance, the leaders would have to learn to integrate the employees of the acquired company into their teams. The HR team may need to integrate the compensation and benefits of the employees from the acquired company. The sales team may need to cross train the frontline sales team on the combined product portfolio.

3. **What is the fastest way to teach people these skills?** The CLO must work out different ways in which these new skill gaps can be bridged in the shortest possible time.

The role of L&D is not just about delivering formal learning in a classroom. The focus should be on enabling employees to excel in their roles.

If the outcome expected is to help employees to build skills that allow career movement by preparing them for a shift to an adjacent role, the L&D team will have to use a different approach. Some organizations are bringing in content from specialized platforms like LinkedIn Learning, Degreed etc. and making it available on their learning platforms.

With a shift from lifetime employment to lifetime employability, the role of learning and development teams will evolve into providing the skills that employees will need to navigate their career choices. The role of corporate L&D will now shift to using Gen AI in helping employees build connections with different ecosystems through which they can prepare themselves for future roles and opportunities. These connections may be present within the organization or outside it and will vary from role to role.

How to build learning agility

Confucius described three approaches to learning. 'First, by reflection, which is the noblest; second, by imitation, which is the easiest; and third by experience, which is the bitterest.'

Learning agility is the ability to continuously learn and adapt to new situations and environments. It is a critical skill for individuals in today's rapidly changing world, as it allows them to stay current in their field, take on new challenges, and adapt to changing circumstances.

There are several ways in which individuals can demonstrate learning agility. Here are a few examples:

- **Seeking out new learning opportunities**: Learning-agile individuals are proactive in seeking out new learning opportunities. This might involve enrolling in courses or workshops, getting a coach or mentor and doing several mini projects that are cross functional and across businesses and geographies.
- **Being open to feedback**: Learning-agile individuals are also open to feedback and willing to learn from their mistakes. They are not afraid to ask for help or seek out guidance from others when they need it.
- **Trying new things**: Learning-agile individuals are not afraid to take risks and try new things, even if it means

stepping out of their comfort zones. This can involve trying new approaches to problem-solving, taking on new roles or responsibilities, or simply exploring new interests and hobbies.

- **Adapting to change**: Finally, learning-agile individuals are able to adapt to change and are not thrown off course when things do not go as planned. They are able to pivot around and find new solutions when faced with challenges or setbacks.

Imagine an individual working in a marketing role at a software company. She is learning-agile, and always looking for ways to improve her skills and stay current in her field. She might take online courses on topics such as data analysis or content marketing, attend industry events and conferences, and seek out mentors or coaches who can provide guidance and support. In addition, she will be open to trying new things and not afraid to take on new projects or roles that require her to learn new skills. For example, she might volunteer to lead a social media campaign or take on a project that involves working with a new marketing platform. By continuously learning and adapting in this way, the individual is able to stay competitive in her field and continue to succeed in her career.

Here's another example: Photography is a constantly evolving field, with new technologies and techniques being developed all the time. As a result, photographers must constantly learn and adapt in order to stay relevant and competitive. They have to learn about new camera equipment and software, as well as keep up with changing trends and styles in the industry. They must learn to leverage Gen AI as an assistant to up their game.

Besides technical skills, photographers also need to continually develop their creative vision and artistic abilities. This can involve studying the work of other photographers, experimenting with new techniques and styles, and continually pushing themselves to improve and grow as artistes. By constantly learning and adapting, photographers can stay at the top of their game and produce work that is fresh and innovative.

Freelance photographers are responsible not only for taking photographs but also for running the business aspects of their photography. This can involve a wide range of tasks, including marketing and promoting their services, managing their finances and budget, and handling administrative tasks such as invoicing and paying taxes.

To be successful as a freelance photographer, it is important to have a good understanding of the business side of photography. This can involve learning about topics such as marketing and branding, financial management and contract negotiation. In addition, freelance photographers may need to develop skills in areas such as customer service and project management, as they may be working with clients directly and coordinating multiple projects at once.

To gain this knowledge and develop these skills, freelance photographers may need to invest time and effort in learning about the business aspects of their art. This could involve taking courses or workshops, reading industry publications and blogs, or seeking guidance from more experienced photographers or business mentors. By learning about the business side of photography, freelance photographers can better manage their careers and succeed as entrepreneurs.

Levels of risk taking, dealing with change and ambiguity

Levels of risk taking, dealing with change, and ambiguity can all significantly shape career paths, as they can affect the choices and opportunities that individuals have available to them.

Those who are willing to take risks may be more likely to pursue careers that involve a high degree of uncertainty or unpredictability. This could include careers in entrepreneurship, where individuals must be willing to take risks to start and grow their own businesses. It could also include careers in the arts, where individuals must be willing to take risks to create and share their work with the world.

On the other hand, those who are less uncomfortable with risk may be more drawn to careers that offer a greater degree of stability and predictability. Careers in the public sector, several government jobs or in large corporations offer stable career paths.

Dealing with change and ambiguity can also shape career paths, as individuals who are more adaptable and comfortable with change may be better suited to careers that involve a high degree of change and uncertainty. This could include careers in fields that are rapidly evolving, such as technology or healthcare, where individuals must be able to adapt to new developments and changing circumstances.

On the other hand, those who struggle with change and ambiguity may be more drawn to careers that offer stability and predictability. This might include careers in fields that are relatively unchanging, such as academia or law, where the rules and procedures are well established and there is less room for ambiguity.

Overall, the level of risk taking, dealing with change and ambiguity that individuals are comfortable with can significantly influence their career paths and the types of jobs and opportunities they pursue. By understanding their own strengths and limitations in these areas, individuals can make informed decisions about the types of careers that are most likely to be a good fit for them.

Art, Business and Craft—the ABC of being self-employed

Joshua Karthik is the co-founder of an internationally renowned wedding photography firm. Acknowledged as an expert in the world of wedding photography, Joshua represents the industry in forums across India and abroad. Over the last ten years, he has had a direct impact on consumer behaviour in this segment through his work in product and business at Stories.

As an educator and mentor, he has worked with hundreds of entrepreneurs in this and allied spaces.

Joshua says, 'A lot of people think of quitting their jobs when things are not going well at work. They want to quit because they have a lousy boss, or because they have been passed over for a promotion or have a colleague they can't stand. None of these is a good reason to quit a job and become self-employed. Instead, quit at a time when you are doing really well as an employee. When I quit Asian Paints after eight years, I was having the time of my life. I had a perfect job, the perfect role, amazing bosses and I worked with a great team. To quit then was the right decision because I could quit with no regrets. My brother Joseph and I have this tendency to ask ourselves what we are going to start next every time we do something really well.'

Joshua quit his job at Asian Paints to join his brother Joseph Radhik as co-founder of 'Stories by Joseph Radhik', Together they have built a winning team of photographers 'who believe in stories; stories of love, laughter and happily ever after'.

With half a billion views for the work they've created, and with 460 shoots in thirty-five countries around the world, Stories has had a significant impact on the wedding photography sector in India and elsewhere. Joshua is also an award-winning photographer, with wins at PX3 Paris, Tokyo Foto Awards and more. You can find him on Instagram and on LinkedIn. If you have seen the wedding photos of Virat Kohli and Anushka Sharma, those photos that broke the Internet were shot by them. As were the photos of Katrina Kaif, Priyanka Chopra-Jonas and many others.

Joshua and Joseph also run a company that educates freelance photographers on the ABC of running a business. ABC stands for Art, Business and Craft.

a. *A for Art*: Art has to do with your vision for what you wish to create. Art is the difference in the way two photographers frame the shot. While most photographers focus on the bride and the groom, one photographer will actually shoot the photo of the father discreetly wiping his tears. Or the aunt who has been invited to the wedding but is ignored. It is what you do outside of the camera that you do with your observation and empathy.

b. *B is for Business:* Business hinges on one skill and not everybody possesses it in equal measure—the skill of dealing with people. If you want to be a gig worker and you want to build or monetize anything, you need people. It is not the quality of your work alone but it is your ability to work with people and to truly build trusting relationships that impacts everything from negotiation to pricing to sales to marketing. It comes back to your ability to work with people.

c. *C for Craft:* Craft is the skill of how you actually put it all together with the tools that you use for your trade. It is a camera for a photographer or a paintbrush and canvas for an artist.

Being self-employed is not for the faint-hearted. There may be several people who are good photographers. Being good at shooting pictures is very different from being good in the business of photography. Today the average smartphone camera is capable of letting every other person post stunning photos. Taking the art of photography beyond the capabilities of the average smartphone is the bigger challenge.

AI-powered softwares like Photoshop have made it possible to make every photo look better. The craftsman behind the lens must do more. When wedding photographers take thousands of photos, someone has to select a smaller number (say, 200 photos) to deliver to the family before the guests leave. Knowing who are the relatives to be given prominence takes a certain amount of observation and judgement. Knowing which photos (and relatives) to ignore takes a colossal amount of emotional intelligence. That is the craft.

Knowing how much to charge is a question that stumps most beginners. The business of photography depends on things like cash flow, profit margins, loans and payables etc. Taxes have to be paid and equipment has to be kept current. The self-employed person must decide how they will get the next assignment. Knowing how to handle clients who cancel the contract at the last moment is crucial. Then there is the need to market the best photos on Instagram. Think of it as snap judgment (pun intended).

The business of photography is not for everyone who is a good photographer. Would you agree?

7

Career 1.0—Learn, Earn and Retire

Career 1.0, also known as the traditional career archetype, is a linear path that has been followed by many professionals for centuries. It involves a three-step process of learn, earn and retire. In this archetype, the person prefers stability in the ecosystem. The employer rewards continuity of employment and creates a pre-defined path with promotions and career growth at fixed intervals. Academic degrees and pedigree of the college are predictors of career success. This has been the dominant career archetype over generations.

The first step in a Career 1.0 is learning. This typically involves obtaining a degree or certification in a specific field, such as medicine or law. In many professions, this is a necessary requirement for pursuing a career in that field. Once an individual has completed his/her education, he/she is ready to move on to the next step: earning.

Earning is the second step in the Career 1.0 archetype. This involves finding a job in the field that an individual has been trained in and beginning to work and earn a salary. In many cases, this is a full-time job that requires a significant amount of dedication and commitment.

The final step in a Career 1.0 is retirement. This is the point at which an individual has reached the end of his/her working years and is ready to leave the job and enjoy the fruits of their labour. For many people, this is a time to relax and enjoy their hobbies and interests, while for others it may involve continuing to work in a different capacity, such as consulting or volunteering.

Career 1.0 was the archetype that emerged when human life spans was around seventy years. These jobs often offer stability and security, as well as a clear path to advancement. They also typically come with a generous retirement package, which allows individuals to retire comfortably and enjoy their golden years.

While Career 1.0 may not be for everyone, it has served as a successful career path for many professionals for centuries. It offers a clear set of steps that individuals can follow to achieve success in their chosen field and provides a sense of stability and security that is often lacking in other career paths. Ultimately, it is up to us to decide whether Career 1.0 is the right path, but for many, it has proven to be a successful and fulfilling career choice.

Career 1.0 offers stability, predictability and low risk

Most parents in India want their children to 'settle down'. That is often shorthand for a stable career. For millions of people in the middle class, a government job is still an aspirational career choice. While the salaries offered by the government do not compare favourably with those offered by private employers, the stability, predictability, power, influence and low risk make a government job a desirable career choice for many.

Jobs in the Indian government are not subject to the same level of market fluctuations as private sector jobs. This means that employees in government jobs can expect a certain level of job security and are less likely to be laid off due to economic downturns or other external factors. Government job descriptions offer a clear set of expectations and responsibilities, which can provide a sense of predictability for employees. People know what they are supposed to do. This can be especially appealing for those who value a sense of structure and routine in their work lives.

A government employee may be able to make decisions that affect the lives of others or shape public policy. For those who like to impact the lives of millions, a government job offers the power and influence necessary to drive changes at scale. A government employee may be able to shape public opinion or influence decision-making processes.

Young Indian Administrative Service (IAS) officers in India often have a lot of responsibility and control when it comes to managing budgets. The IAS is a prestigious and competitive civil service in India, and those who are selected to become IAS officers are typically given a wide range of responsibilities and duties. One of these responsibilities is managing budgets. IAS officers may be responsible for managing budgets for entire departments or for specific programmes or projects. These budgets can be quite large, often running into crores of rupees.

Managing budgets requires a lot of skill and expertise, as it involves making decisions about how to allocate resources and allocate funds in the most effective and efficient way possible. IAS officers must be able to analyse financial data and make informed decisions based on their analysis.

In addition to managing budgets, IAS officers may also be responsible for a wide range of other duties, including implementing government policies and programmes, managing personnel, and working with stakeholders to achieve their goals.

Government jobs are often considered low risk when it comes to the possibility of getting laid off. Many government jobs come with a certain level of tenure, which means that employees can only be terminated for certain specific reasons, such as misconduct or poor performance. This can provide a sense of security for employees, as they know that they cannot be arbitrarily laid off. In India, government employees are often protected by the civil service protection laws, which provide additional safeguards against lay-offs and other forms of job insecurity.

Some government jobs in India are unionized, which means that employees are represented by a union and have additional protection against lay-offs and other forms of job insecurity.

Government jobs in essential services, such as healthcare and public safety, are often considered more secure because these services must be maintained even during economic downturns. Jobs with the police, army, navy and air force offer a great combination of a stable career and great perks.

The downside of stability, predictability and low risk-taking

Government jobs can often be quite rigid, with strict rules and regulations governing how work is performed. This may not be appealing to those who value flexibility in their work lives. Promotions are based on tenure, and it is hard for most people to get promoted ahead of their peers. This may be frustrating for those who want to move up the ladder quickly.

Government jobs may also be limited in terms of opportunities for innovation and creativity. This may not be appealing to those who want to be at the forefront of new ideas and technologies. These jobs may also be subject to bureaucracy and red tape, which can be frustrating for those who want to get things done quickly and efficiently.

My career path started with Career 1.0 and then . . .

Once I completed my master in personnel management and industrial relations from XLRI—Xavier School of Management Jamshedpur, it was time to make a choice. Would it be better to be a generalist or a specialist? It was hard to choose. When that choice was made for me, I was relieved. I joined my first job as a personnel executive at Eicher GoodEarth Limited, as part of the campus placement. It was my first foray into corporate India. I had also signed up to do a bachelor's degree in law but had no desire to practice it. I was happy exploring various aspects of my field. But later, having acquired a degree in Law, I wanted to apply it as part of my job.

Managing industrial relations (IR) for a factory that had a history of conflict and litigation with five trade unions seemed like a logical choice for me. Being part of the IR team at Shalimar Paints on the outskirts of Kolkata gave me my first taste of being a specialist. But this was not a specialization I wanted to pursue further. It was then that my boss, S.D. Barman (not the music composer), suggested I should explore a career in training and development.

The Management Development Centre of Tata Steel was headed by Jittu Singh, who was my professor at XLRI. His advice and mentorship shaped my professional DNA and built my love for the learning and development function. The office, located next to the XLRI campus, gave me an opportunity to co-author a white paper with some professors of XLRI. They invited me to teach part-time at some of the management development programmes that XLRI offered to working executives. I also taught training and development to the students at XLRI. It was like discovering my sweet tooth! I spent five years at this dessert counter. I discovered that I enjoyed being a specialist—in the emerging field of learning and development. Getting paid by XLRI to teach didn't hurt either. I had unknowingly become part of the Career 2.0 tribe.

Mudra, a well-known ad agency, was setting up a business school in Ahmedabad to train professionals in communications. Many years later, I was invited to be a part of the Governing Council of MICA, formerly known as Mudra Institute of Communications, Ahmedabad. Being the head of HR for Mudra gave me a chance to understand the world of advertising professionals, an experience that I could build upon when social media and tech started changing the world.

Colgate Palmolive was looking for an HR person to implement their human resources information system. This role took me to work for them in Mumbai, Kuala Lumpur and Malaysia. Later, while working for COlage in the US, I ran a radio show about movies and music from the Bollywood of the 1970s. I didn't really get paid for this side hustle. But soon, I was back to following a Career 1.0 path even though I changed several employers. If anyone asked me, 'What do you do for a living?' I would say, "I am an human resources professional.' That was my identity and remained so for several years.

I worked as a generalist in human resources while at PepsiCo. My role as the chief learning officer (CLO) at Wipro was a more specialized one. Learning and development offers many opportunities for specialization within human resources. Talent acquisition, compensation, benefits, HR analytics, HR operations etc. are all roles held by specialists.

After a few years of being the CLO, I tried my hand at launching my own consulting firm. We were a small firm of six associates who specialized in three areas—leadership, talent and culture. Our clients ranged from Fortune 500 firms to small start-ups and even individuals. This is when I experienced Career 3.0 where I was monetizing my consulting assignments, being a brand influencer for global firms like Adobe and SHRM, getting paid to host my podcasts and writing books and keynotes. I was living the dream.

In 2022, I was invited by Microsoft to head their global learning and development team based out of the US. I started my life on the traditional Career 1.0 path and moved to 3.0 and at Microsoft, am now pursuing a Career 1.0 path again.

People move in and out of these three archetypes. Career 1.0 is not worse than the Career 2.0 path. Career 3.0 is not superior to the Career 2.0 archetype. At different times, one will come to the forefront and the others

Work—worker—workplaces

In my book *Dreamers and Unicorns: How Leadership, Talent and Culture are the New Growth Drivers* (Westland 2020), I spoke about work, workers and workplaces being intricately connected. A change in any one of them will force a change in the other two. The way work gets done dictates the skills that are needed. People who have the necessary skills form the talent pool of workers, who shape the norms of the workplace. Historically, these changes have happened in sequence with the change in the way of working, leading to a change in the people who can do the work. Workplaces have evolved in response to changes in the work and worker.

Before the Industrial Revolution, agriculture employed a lot of people. The First Industrial Revolution changed the way we worked. Steam powered the machines in the factories, requiring a new set of workers whose skills were different from those of the workers who continued to work in the fields. The factory had become the new workplace. A hundred years later, electricity changed the way of working. Assembly lines in the factory allowed for mass production. Electricity made it possible to keep the factories working even after sunset. Shift working needed shift supervisors. The workplace had changed to respond to the new workforce and the new method of working.

The telecom revolution has made it possible for work to be done from anywhere. It was during the pandemic that we saw seismic shifts in work, workers and workplaces simultaneously. During this period, we discovered that work could be done from any place that had connectivity. Home became the new workplace. The lines between what was personal and what belonged to the workplace got blurred. The pandemic and now Gen AI are redefining the workplace. Gen AI will soon be the invisible assistant every employee will have. Until the pandemic, we believed that everyone needed to be present simultaneously in one physical location—the workplace and have common hours of work. This was an assumption that had not been challenged. The ability to 'unlearn' is to give up a mental model that is no longer relevant in the current context. The debate about mandatory return to office is a good example of the unlearning that is needed by the employer and the employees. Unlearning is like an addiction that is hard to shake off.

The bosses wanted to utilize the office spaces that had been built with the assumption that everyone comes in to work at the *same time and in the same place*. The workers wanted to continue to avail themselves of the flexibility of time and place of work. Once again, the equilibrium between work, worker and workplace has been uprooted. Till the new equilibrium is found, the tension will continue. The new equation of work–

worker–workplace will have to be co-created. This may be the first day in a five-year cycle of evolution. The norms of the workplace will have to be co-created.

How technology changes work, the worker and the workplace

The mobile revolution changed work. It allowed us to be untethered from our desk. Work could be carried home on the mobile phone. This changed the talent pool. Telecom companies boomed, the iPhone became a thing and smartphones evolved from being status symbols to functional pieces of technology. App development became a career choice for millions. It changed business models across sectors—from media and entertainment to telemedicine, transportation and ecommerce. The list of the biggest Fortune 500 companies reflected the change. Technology companies started dominating the list of the biggest, fastest growing and most sought-after career makers.

Technology has had a significant impact on work, the worker and the workplace in recent years. As new technologies have emerged and become widely adopted, they have transformed the way that work is done and the skills that are required to be successful in the workplace.

One way that technology has changed work is by automating tasks and processes that were previously done by humans. This has led to the emergence of new job roles, such as data scientists and machine learning engineers, as well as the decline of jobs that are easily automated. At the same time, technology has also made it possible for workers to perform their jobs remotely, allowing them to work from anywhere with an Internet connection. This has led to a shift towards flexible and remote work arrangements, which can offer greater work-life balance and convenience to workers.

Technology has also changed the worker by increasing the speed at which work can be done and the amount of information that can be processed. This has led to a greater demand for workers who are able to adapt to new technologies and learn new skills quickly. It has also increased the importance of soft skills, such as communication and collaboration, as workers are often required to work with others remotely or across different time zones.

In terms of the workplace, technology has changed the way that people interact with each other and with their work environment. For example, the widespread adoption of video conferencing has made it possible for people to have face-to-face meetings without being in the same physical location. At the same time, the use of social media and other online platforms has made it easier for people to connect and collaborate with each other, even when they are not in the same place.

Overall, technology has had a significant impact on work, the worker, and the workplace, and it is likely to continue to do so in the future. As technology continues to advance and change, it is important for workers to stay up to date and adapt to the changing landscape of work.

Most changes in the world of work are continuous i.e., perpetual beta

From business models to skill changes, the world of work is seeing a shift from episodic changes to changes that are more continuous and almost invisible. Employee engagement is no longer measured by annual surveys. The ability to learn something is no longer measured by degrees but by the ability to learn different skills over the span of one's career.

The job descriptions folder in many organizations in India used to be updated by interns. The jobs did not change that often. But now, three major reasons for changing job descriptions are:

1. **Changes in the job itself:** As a company or organization evolves, the tasks and responsibilities of a particular job may change. This could be due to changes in the company's business model, new technologies or processes that are implemented, or shifts in the company's goals or objectives. As a result, the job description may need to be updated to reflect these changes.

2. **Changes in the external environment:** Changes in the external environment, such as shifts in the industry or changes in customer needs, can also lead to changes in job descriptions. For example, if a company is facing increased competition, it may need to adapt its business model or add new products or services to stay competitive. This could result in changes being made in job descriptions as the company seeks to hire workers with the skills and experience needed to support these changes.

3. **Changes in the internal organization:** Job descriptions and roles can also change because of changes in the internal organization of a company. This could include restructuring or reorganization of the company, changes in leadership, or the introduction of new policies or procedures. These changes can impact the tasks and responsibilities related to a particular job and may require the job description to be updated.

The world of work keeps evolving. So do the rules of success. The role of a people manager has changed dramatically in the post-pandemic world. Trying to keep the team intact in a world of rising inflation and limited budgets is extremely hard. It is much easier to hand over a promotion letter to a grateful employee than it is to tell someone that their performance is below standard. Managing an experienced group of employees requires a very different managerial skill set compared to the skills needed to manage employees at the start of their career. Being able to earn the trust of the team of specialists and experts can be very different from managing a team of novices. When someone gets promoted to lead and manager, the employees who were once peers can become very demanding. When organizations ask employees to bring their whole self to work, the role of the manager increases in complexity. They now need to be able to demonstrate understanding towards a top performer who may have polarizing political views. Building an inclusive culture requires tremendous emotional involvement and time commitment that people underestimate when they take on a leadership role. 'This is not what I expected to do' is a reaction more common than you think.

Careers in perpetual beta

In conclusion, the concept of 'perpetual beta' suggests that careers should never be considered fully 'finished' and should always be in a state of continuous improvement. This approach is becoming increasingly relevant in today's rapidly changing job market, where workers are expected to adapt to new technologies and changing industry demands.

Embracing a perpetual beta mindset can help us stay current and competitive in our careers. This may involve continuously learning new skills and staying current with changes in the industry, as well as being open to new opportunities and challenges.

In order to succeed in a career in perpetual beta, it is important for workers to be proactive and take ownership of their own development. This may involve seeking out training and education, networking with others in their field, and actively seeking out new opportunities for growth and advancement.

CAREER 1.0   ONE SKILL DEPLOYED IN ONE ECOSYSTEM

PROFICIENCY IS BUILT
THROUGH REPETITION

SENIORITY DENOTES
GREATER EXPERTISE

RECOMMEND:
STAY ADAPTABLE BY ADDING
TO YOUR SKILL REGULARLY

I PREFER A VET WHO SPECIALIZES
IN TREATING FEROCIOUS DOGS

 @ABHIJITBHADURI
#CAREER3

Career 1.0 is common to gamers and flair bartenders

It is tempting to believe that Career 1.0 is limited to traditional career choices. That could not be farther from the truth.

In emerging fields like gaming, the skill and the ecosystem are evolving at a rapid pace. The games business is international: last year's twenty highest grossing mobile games came from nine countries. The gaming ecosystem is already bigger than movies and sports. Games like *Candy Crush*, *Roblox* or *Pokémon* that were designed in the US already generate more than a billion dollars of revenue each. A game like *Honor of Kings* generates close to \$3 billion for China. The gaming ecosystem offers plenty of options to thrive in a Career 1.0 archetype.

Management consulting firm Korn Ferry reports say that an average tech worker receives seventeen emails every month from recruiters. A specialist, on the other hand, gets almost 200 calls from recruiters. So, is it a good career strategy to become a specialist? Is that what the Career 1.0 career archetype is all about? Let's tease out the nuances of that choice.

Most professions have generalists and specialists. The generalists do several things in limited doses. They focus on building breadth. The specialist does a few things but over times builds ability in one narrow area of interest. A career in Law can supply many opportunities. Some may choose to be employed by a firm, while others may prefer to be apprentices to a more established lawyer as they learn the ropes.

The line between specialists and generalists is getting blurred. A general physician is a generalist. That is an easy one to understand. What about a doctor of internal medicine or family medicine? A dentist is a generalist, but orthodontics is a definite specialization.

Any aspect of our life that gets governed by the legal system offers opportunities for specialization. Lawyers can offer counsel on human rights, animal rights, property and estate matters, intellectual property, immigration law, civil law, criminal law, maritime law, company law, constitutional law . . . the list is endless. Within each field, there are lawyers who specialize further. These super-specializations are often combinations of multiple disciplines. Medico-legal advice is an example of this super specialization.

It has becoming increasingly difficult to define where one discipline ends and another one begins.

Career 1.0 is about monetizing one skill in one ecosystem.

There are three elements that form the basis of our career choices:

1. The skills acquired through formal education
2. The skills that are self-taught
3. The choice of the employer or the ecosystem

Career 1.0 is about monetizing one skill or educational qualification in one ecosystem. Quite often, the employer tries to discourage employees from pursuing any other sources of income. Schools and colleges often look the other way when they know that the teacher offers private tuition. Hospitals know that some of the best doctors pursue thriving private practices. This is the grey zone that bridges Career 1.0 with the Career 2.0 archetype.

Sometimes people create a unique combination of skills that makes them the sole player in a field of one—like flair bartending. A flair bartender is a bartender who juggles cocktail shakers and liquor bottles in tricky, dazzling ways. Think of it like a bartender who used to be a juggler until last week. Flair bartending is sometimes referred to as 'extreme bartending' or contracted to 'flairtending'.

When Ami Shroff was studying philosophy and political science in college, she had no idea that there was a career path possible as a flair bartender. She combines her passion for juggling and mixing cocktails to be a flair bartender. This is a great example of combining different skills to create a unique combination. Is that a Career 1.0 path as purists would define it? Her LinkedIn profile describes her as 'India's 1st female flair bartender, mixologist and performing artist since 2003'.

Education used to create lifetime employability for people. That was the dominant model for most people, especially those who worked for an employer. Career was all about finding a job that ensured stability and predictability. Even promotions had to follow a predictable pattern. A person who had joined the employer a few days earlier could continue to stay ahead simply by way of that 'seniority'.

Experience is valued in Career 1.0 jobs. Doing the job for more years improves ability on the job. The surgeon who has performed a hundred surgeries is likely to be more skilled than the newcomer. The trainee pilot needs to clock in several hours of flying to build up ability. Single-minded focus defines this career path. An excellent job in this archetype is one that is characterized by focus and minimal change. Most jobs in the government and public sector offer these working conditions. Once hired, the employees have a clear view of their career path, pay hikes and promotions. For many people, a job with the government is a coveted outcome.

This summarizes the career journey for most people who are not managing their own business. Running a business was a privilege offered usually to those born within a business family. The rest had to find a job before they could 'settle down'—a euphemism for predictability. The middle class of India valued power and predictability. The government job was understandably coveted. Job security mattered to a nation where wages were low and social security was what the family could rustle up. The public sector and the bureaucracy in most countries work like well-oiled machines. During times of National Emergency in India, we have seen how the state machinery swung into action and restored normalcy in a noticeably short span of time. This happens because the procedures, once developed, can be replicated and adapted by the states.

Routine, stability and predictability are slowly disappearing

Career 1.0 offers stability and predictability. Everything moves according to predetermined rules, with limited opportunities to shine and differentiate oneself. The army is a good example of this kind of career preference. In this career stage, there are three distinct phases—learning, earning and retiring.

a) Learning: Getting the academic qualifications necessary to find employment.

b) Earning: The years of employment with one or more employers. These years are marked with a fair degree of predictability in earnings. The years of experience become valuable because the skills needed to do the work remain stable. Each year of experience deepens the ability of the employee. The employer handles the upgradation of skills. Skill upgradation is rewarded through promotions.

c) Retiring: When an employee achieves a certain age, they retire from active service. For most people, it is a time to put their feet up and look back on a life well lived. They enjoy the relaxed pace of their sunset years.

The three-step model has not gone away. It still appeals to a lot of people who step into the workforce today. It is a particularly attractive option for people who like stability more than constant change and adaptation. Employers who are shielded from market forces can offer a stable employment experience. The jobs offered by the state and central government and several public sector employers continue to offer stability and a pre-determined career route map for every employee. Even in this cocoon, the market forces are shoehorning their way in. Public sector companies are being privatized and several arms of government departments are being outsourced to private operators. Several services in the railways and defence ministries are offered to contractors who can bid for these opportunities.

Career 1.0 will remain a choice for many people, but there is a growing tribe of people who believe that doing a side hustle is fun.

Serendipity plays a part too

Julia Child was an American chef, author and television personality who was born in Pasadena, California. She began her career as a research assistant at the Office of Strategic Services during World War II, but she later became interested in cooking and attended the Cordon Bleu cooking school in Paris. Child became a successful chef and television personality, and she is credited with introducing French cuisine to the world through her cookbook, *Mastering the Art of French Cooking* and her television show, *The French Chef*. But Julia Child is not the only one to switch her career path.

Shah Rukh Khan is an actor, film producer and television host from India. He studied economics in college. Steve Jobs trained as a physicist and a computer scientist, but he became better known as the co-founder of Apple. Rakesh Jhunjhunwala was an Indian investor and trader. He was initially trained as a chartered accountant, but he became better known for his work in the field of stock trading and investing. He started Akasa Airlines before he passed away.

J.K. Rowling was initially trained as a researcher and a bilingual secretary but is better known as the author of the *Harry Potter* series. Ratan Tata, chairman emeritus of Tata Sons, was initially trained as an architect.

A crisis is an opportunity to get creative about your career

In many societies, children as young as fourteen or fifteen are expected to choose the academic stream that will impact their choice of college and undergraduate degree. The undergraduate degree in turn shapes the options they have for further studies or going to work. It is only after they have worked for a couple of years, that they pause to ask themselves if the work that they are doing is what they really wanted to do. When that happens in the first decade of our careers, we call it a quarter-life crisis. When it happens in our forties, we call it a mid-life crisis.

We sometimes pause to ask ourselves, 'Am I successful at work?'

If we feel that we are not as successful as our peers, we may contemplate changing jobs. Sometimes we think of adding to our skills and seeking greener pastures.

We sometimes pause to ask ourselves, 'Am I happy? Is this what creates meaning in my life?'

These are deeper questions that cannot be resolved by changing jobs. They have very little to do with where we are with respect to our peers.

When we feel overwhelmed with too many choices or feel anxious about our lack of choices, we think of it as a 'crisis'.

A crisis is a tap on our shoulder that reminds us to pause and recalibrate our lives. Sometimes the side gig is an opportunity to sample what the alternative career path can offer. Doing the side hustle can be a way to deepen one's expertise before taking it to the talent marketplace. So, when someone in your workplace invites you to try out a short-term project, grab the opportunity to try it out. Many people view cross-functional moves to broaden their skills without changing employers.

Maybe you should consider a move from Career 1.0 to Career 2.0.

8

Career 2.0: Two Skills Monetized in Two Different Ecosystems

Career 2.0 is about people who have made dramatic shifts in their career path. There are many ways in which people can monetize a second skill. Sometimes they change careers altogether. The person who is trained in one profession can acquire new educational qualifications that let them succeed in their new professional path. Sometimes this is achieved by practising a hobby and spending 10,000 hours perfecting it until there are people willing to pay for that skill. Monetization is proof of proficiency.

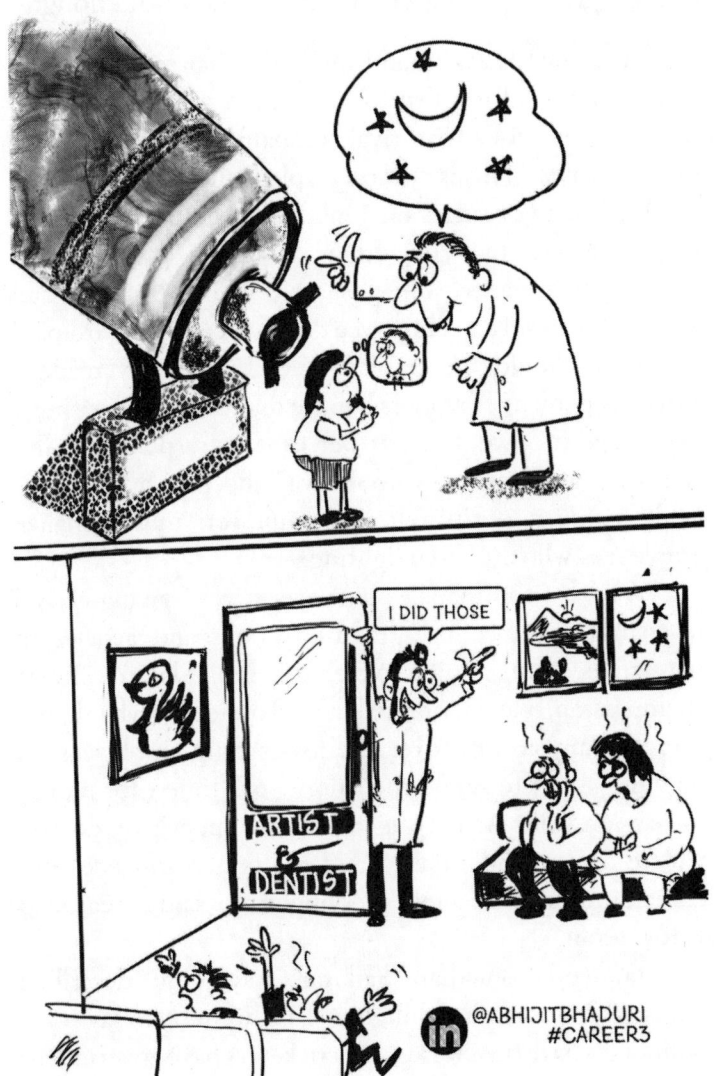

Moonlighting is a sign that Career 1.0 is not enough

Sometime in 2022, Rishad Premji, the chairman of Indian tech and consulting firm Wipro, fired 300 workers for taking second jobs with rival companies. He described it on Twitter as, 'This is cheating—plain and simple.'

I asked my readers on LinkedIn if employers should let employees take up other paid jobs if it doesn't impact performance? The post went viral with more than 1,71,000 views. If an employee does a second or third paid job, what should the employer do, I asked my readers. Fifty-six percent of readers believe that the employer must encourage it. Twenty-eight per cent of respondents felt that the employers must look away and turn a blind eye. Only a tiny minority felt that employers must penalize employees who are moonlighting.

'We have top management executives—giving classes in management colleges, writing books and articles in magazines, acting as directors on other boards, etc.—living their passion, one-off or regular, paid or not. So why should there be any control over the lower rung employees on how they want to spend their non-work time—for money or passion/skill? As long as it is non-competitive, doesn't violate data confidentiality, and meets performance, etc., companies need to allow moonlighting,' said a seasoned HR veteran.

Stand-up comedian Saikiran Rayaprolu described India as a 'nation of moonlighters'. He went on to say, 'Our politicians have businesses, our cricketers have government jobs, our doctors and teachers have clinics and tuitions. When the side hustle of most employees was mutual funds, real estate, cryptocurrency, cricket betting etc., it was okay, but the moment they start using their *actual* skills to earn some extra income, all hell breaks loose.'

Several CEOs are on the board of directors in other companies, advisors to NGOs, part of some government panel or an industry body like NASSCOM, formerly known as National Association of Software and Service Companies.

People invest money in the stock market to build financial security. They trade, they invest, and many earn from them, all during office hours. Some earn so much that they need to pay taxes for that.

Some people are unclear about what career paths to choose. Their college degrees often do not reflect a career choice that they are fully committed to. Hence the side hustle alongside their regular career.

In his own words—Sumit Saurav—from campus to campusdiaries.com

I grew up in Jamshedpur and Ranchi. I took up engineering almost as a pre-ordained choice—it was the default option. I was not very clear about why I was doing what I was doing. I changed my field of engineering five times and finally settled for the electrical engineering branch.

I was much busier outside the classroom than inside. I was part of a band, organized the college festival and represented my university in middle-distance running.

When it came to finding internships, I struggled to find opportunities that fit my interests and personality. This is where students from the metros and larger cities have an advantage. Their families would step in to help find them internships. Even the students had a clear view about the kind of internships that would be viewed favourably by a future employer.

From these frustrations and anxieties was born the idea of campusdiaries.com—a platform for students, where they could express their interests and find opportunities that matched their personality and preferences. The platform connected over 1,00,000 students across India. I had solved a problem for so many people, but my start-up failed because I could not find a way to monetize the idea. What stayed with me was my interest and skills in connecting culture and design.

In the next phase, I became a consultant and helped organizations across the globe in developing community-led platforms, products and experiences. In the past five years, I have worked with a variety of communities and spaces. I have worked with farmers, connecting them with digital marketplaces. I worked with HR and business leaders to help them shape the organizational culture with their employees. I worked with consumer product companies to help them create participatory research and insights.

Currently, Sumit leads a platform called Chance Labs which takes 'jobs of the future' to Bharat (small town and rural India). They have turned homemakers, with only a school education, into AI analysts. Sumit is part of the movement that is creating opportunities in the digital marketplace for tier-two and tier-three cities in India.

Career 2.0—two skills, two income streams, two ecosystems

Case: Madhulika Ra Chauhan

Sometimes careers aren't something that you plan, instead it is life which charts one's moves while one is busy planning one's next. Madhulika's journey has been outlined and punctuated with interesting twists and turns.

After a bachelor of business administration from Meerut University, Madhulika came to Delhi to pursue a master's in IT from the India Institute of Planning and Management. This was at the turn of the century when the dotcom bubble had burst.

The outsourcing industry was booming, and it gave Madhulika her first career break. The outsourcing and research firms where she spent the first few years prepared her for a stint as a media analyst at EY. She loved her job and felt that satisfaction she had been looking for, for the past few years. She describes it as 'a phase of learning and growing'.

And then life happened. She got married.

Soon enough, her husband got a job offer from his firm to go to China and Madhulika had to become the proverbial trailing spouse. Her employer offered her a six-month sabbatical which she decided to use to learn about the culture, rituals and possibilities in her new home. While that seemed like a unique experience, the language barrier would stump her at every step. 'It can overwhelm even the most enthusiastic person,' she said. She used the six-month sabbatical to explore the city and even auditioned as a news reader for local channels and learnt Chinese painting.

Meanwhile her husband's company extended his stay. The six-month sabbatical from her employer would not cover this new set of circumstances. Determined not to give up, she joined IBM in China in December 2007 as a language trainer. She did not find a position in research (which she had done for years and was good at) and instead took the opportunity that came her way. A manager from the quality team noticed her creative problem-solving skills and invited her to join the quality assurance team. That meant studying to get additional qualifications. Madhulika became a black belt in Lean Six Sigma.

And then life happened again. Her son was born in 2010.

Incredibly, the birth of her son triggered her creative instinct. She discovered her passion for creative writing. Initially she viewed it just as a passing phase but soon the daily practice of creative writing improved her craft. Her friends and family encouraged her to write to publishers and ask if they would be interested in publishing her work. Her book of short stories was released in 2014. It created a new identity for Madhulika. She was a certified Lean Six Sigma professional with a steady career in quality and a published author.

In 2015, she joined the core team of a not-for-profit firm working in the field of women's health, sanitation and environment. She managed to forge associations with the United Nations Water, Sanitation and Hygiene initiatives for which she was awarded the Pravasi Bharatiya Puraskar in 2018.

Today, she is fascinated with short form videos. She loves creating content on topics as diverse as Lean Six Sigma, mythology and green energy. Does she find these subjects disjointed and disconnected?

'I believe that all fields and subjects are interconnected at a very fundamental level. They solve human problems, but every subject uses a different lens,' says Madhulika.

Case: Shaun Eli Breidbart

Shaun Eli Breidbart had a degree from Wharton and was a banker on Wall Street for nineteen years. He knew he had a flair for comedy because he was already writing jokes and selling them freelance to the late-night talk show hosts Jay Leno, Jimmy Fallon, and Conan O'Brien. Then he decided to take a class on how to write and perform stand-up comedy. He would try to go on stage five or six times a week. Six years after he started stand-up comedy, he could truthfully declare that he had two full-time jobs. He quit his job as a banker and shifted to being a full-time comedian—a profession that pays much less than what he used to make as a Wall Street banker.[*]

Career 2.0 is not the same as multi-tasking

Career 2.0 is not about multi-tasking; it is about learning and monetizing two or more different skills in two ecosystems. Parents instruct their children to hold a job and manage the house. Each one of these tasks needs different skills, but only one of them is being monetized. Monetization is not the only reason people work; but this framework will focus on the trend of more than one skill that brings in an additional source of income. The definitions can get blurry.

When a farmer grows produce and sells it, two distinct skills are being used—farming and selling. The parent who was once a professional singer and who now supplements the family income by selling homemade sweets, having monetized two skills, can also be defined as a Career 2.0 archetype. When someone gets promoted from being an individual contributor to managing a team, they are using vastly different skills, and both have been monetized at different points of time in their career.

In India, a number of sectors force people to look for a second source of income because the first one does not pay enough. Many people who work on their own farms move to urban areas to make money because their income from

---

[*] Louis, Pierre-Antoine, 'A Wall Street Banker Turned to Comedy for Happiness and a Career Change', *New York Times*, 21 December, 2021. https://www.nytimes.com/2021/12/21/style/banker-comedian-shaun-eli-breidbart.html, accessed on August 4, 2023.

agriculture is inadequate. While Career 2.0 recognizes this as a distinct skill and monetization combination, the second skill can get monetized simultaneously or create a different career path at a different stage in life.

Think of Career 2.0 as having a side gig in a different ecosystem, that brings in a consistent income stream from a distinctly different skill. Hourly workers have historically supplemented low wages by creating an alternative source of income. Some professions that do not pay enough force people to make ends meet by monetizing another skill. Many schoolteachers and college professors offer tuition and that generates funds. Sometimes the second gig is done out of compulsion, but it is equally possible for the second gig to be a way of nurturing one's dream.

Driving for Uber or Lyft, food delivery, dog walking etc. have become increasingly common ways to earn some more or a way to fund a vacation or a dream home.

The Career 2.0 archetype describes the employee who nurtures her passion in parallel until one day she makes the switch to pursue it full-time. The engineer, who has been a weekend chef, finally gathers the courage to switch careers. Career 2.0 also involves an element of entrepreneurial energy to create a market for the skill being monetized. The medical doctor who forms a professional band is pursuing a Career 2.0 path.

Case: An architect who is a pottery designer

Varsha Chella, based in Chennai, is an architect who discovered pottery. As an architect, she looks at spaces and carves out rooms and other living spaces from that emptiness. Pottery helps her visualize her creations in clay.

Varsha was always a curious and inquisitive person, who enjoyed learning purely for the joy of it. At an early age, she discovered her passion for art and worked steadily throughout her teen years to hone her skills. Her ability to conceptualize spatial ideas and communicate them visually led her to study architecture in Chennai.

She was thoroughly engaged by the complexity of space planning and enjoyed the challenge of creating visually and experientially rich spaces against a framework of rigid functional demands. During her fourth year of architecture, she completed a year-long internship at one of the most prestigious firms in the country—Mancini Enterprises. Her experience at Mancini Enterprises expanded her understanding of the scope of work of an architect. She realized that the principles of 'architectural design thinking' could be applied to a wide array of tangible, functional objects, like furniture, lighting, customized products, fabrics and soft furnishing, and so on.

Having gained this new widened perspective, Varsha stumbled upon the work of Hungarian industrial designer Eva Zeisel. She was thoroughly inspired by the designer's fresh approach to the ceramic medium and so she decided to try her hand at the same. Varsha believed that while architects get to design objects that are executed by others, ceramics gave her the chance to not only design, but also bring her designs to life, and she was curious to explore this new perspective.

'Working at the potter's wheel is a humbling experience. You have to learn to listen to the material and understand that. It helped me develop empathy and also impacted my approach to architecture. I could view the potential of the craftsmen in the team and that empathy changes the way I design,' she says.

Varsha soon realized that she had an aptitude for making ceramics. She spent the first few years mastering her skills in ceramics, without seeking to sell the pottery that she had created. Over the last few years, she has harnessed her potential as a designer to create fresh and original ceramic pieces that bring out the beauty and the inherent qualities of the ceramic material.

Varsha now posts her work on Instagram @Varsha_Chella. Selling on Instagram requires building an authentic connection with the community by sharing more of yourself. And she has done it successfully.

Varsha is now engaged in combining her insight into the world of architecture, with her skill and expertise in ceramics to create a line of 'Architectural Ceramics' for various applications in buildings and interiors. What would she advise people who wish to pursue a Career 2.0 option?

She talks about three stages:

1. Build your expertise and don't be in a hurry to monetize it.
2. Build the community around your work. Showcase the process of creation.
3. Monetization happens when the community believes you have the expertise to deliver a flawless product.

Varsha is based in Chennai and works on creative commissions across disciplines like architecture, interiors, product design, ceramics and illustrations. How does the future look, I asked her.

'I will continue to be an architect. I want to find a way to do whatever the creative urge pushes me to do. Ceramics is just one interpretation of the craft. Tomorrow it could be glass or metal or anything else,' she replied.

Career 2.0 moves centre stage

Fast Internet connections coupled with the acceptance of remote work, specialized platforms that created the marketplace for skills, social media that made it easy to upload and share a video to the world and the payment gateways that made it easy to get paid enabled many people to experiment with a side gig. One in five adults in the UK is involved in another job besides their main occupation, according to a survey conducted by Aviva.[*]

A survey by Kantar in 2023 shows that 30 per cent of the workforce have a second job due to economic concerns, with GenZ being the most impacted group with 40 per cent having two or more roles. The trend of having a 'side hustle' spans across generations, including 36 per cent of millenials, 30 per cent of Gen X and 21 per cent boomers. According to the World Economic Forum, the side hustle is a growing trend in India.[†]

---

[*] Anon, 'One in Five Brits Have Started a "Side Hustle" since March 2020', Aviva, 13 June 2022, https://www.aviva.com/newsroom/news-releases/2022/06/one-in-five-brits-have-started-a-side-hustle-since-march-2020/, accessed 16 July 2023.

[†] Sharma, Niharika, 'Why Are Side Hustles Becoming a Growing Trend in India?', WEForum, 17 March 2022, https://www.weforum.org/agenda/2022/03/india-companies-employees-side-hustle-work/, accessed 16 July 2023.

Social connections, recognition, extra income, a way to create meaning and comfort with social media all come together to create new career opportunities that would have been impossible just a few years back. Career shifts can be triggered by failure. Amitabh Bachchan got rejected as a radio announcer but went on to become the most recognizable voice of India. A career path is as unique as a fingerprint. Many people juggle more than one income stream arising from a second unique skill. This is the second career archetype. Most employers ignore an employee's hobbies or skills if it cannot be used on the job right away. Most frown upon it as a distraction that must be tolerated. The The motives may vary, but this archetype will remain.

Why do a second job?

Labour laws in India and most employers frown upon full-time employees running their own business on the side or even working part-time for someone else. Staying away from the office during the pandemic provided people the option to try out a side hustle. The Great Resignation gave people a chance to re-evaluate their career goals and aspirations. They wanted to de-risk themselves as examples of lay offs filled newspaper headlines.

Why do a second job? According to a study by ResumeBuilder, 69 per cent of remote workers are working a second job; 37 per cent of remote workers have a second full-time job, and 32 per cent have a side hustle.[*]

---

[*] '7 in 10 Remote Workers Have Multiple Jobs', Resume Builder 19 January 2023, https://www.resumebuilder.com/7-in-10-remote-workers-have-multiple-jobs/, accessed 16 July 2023.

WHY DO PEOPLE FIND A SECOND JOB
SOME JOBS SIMPLY DON'T PAY ENOUGH
SOME JOBS ARE JUST NOT INSPIRING

A SECOND JOB CAN BE A GREAT WAY TO
1. LEARN NEW SKILLS
2. FIND NEW NETWORKS
3. FIND JOB SATISFACTION

EMPLOYERS CAN CREATE SHORT-TERM PROJECTS TO ENCOURAGE CAREER 2.0

@ABHIJITBHADURI #CAREER3

1. **Some jobs do not pay enough:** Composer Philip Sheppard shocked a room full of listeners on Clubhouse when he said that the lead trumpet player of an upcoming James Bond movie also delivers packages for Amazon to make ends meet. It is commonplace for teachers to supplement their salaries through private tuitions.

2. **Managing financial risk:** Employees can be laid off with very little warning, forcing numerous families on the brink of poverty. A second job or a side gig is an insurance policy. Some tech workers must take a salary drop to be able to work from a location of their choice. They make up the difference with their second or third 'jobs'.

3. **The main job is not inspiring enough:** For many people, the day job they have been forced to continue doing is uninspiring. The side job provides them the meaning that the main job does not. The second job can simply be a way to find meaning. Magsaysay award winner Anshu Gupta is the founder of an Indian based non-profit—Goonj. One of India's leading social entrepreneurs Anshu studied mass communication and economics. He worked for Chaitra, Power Grid and Escorts 1998 and founded GOONJ with a mission to make clothing a matter of concern and to bring it among the list of subjects for the development sector. His mission was to address the most basic but ignored need of clothing and the multifaceted role it plays in villages across India.

4. **Employers do it all the time:** 'When my company sends projects to India, it is called outsourcing. I outsource my designs to designers in low wage countries. They get paid more than their local rates. I get to work with the best,' says a designer. Most of the people she outsources the designs to have full-time jobs as designers. They do it to build their portfolio, to learn from the other designers and make some money in the process.

5. **Common practice in many professions:** A well-known composer was not given the Oscar because he could not prove that the music for the film was created by him. He is known to use many struggling musicians to create the score and then buy the rights to the music. Some 'prolific authors' use ghost writers to churn out novel.

6. **Skill building opportunity**: The second job can be a powerful way for people to build skills without the employer having to send them off to a training programme. Some organizations reward employees with entrepreneurial skills by adding them to the firm's list of vendors when the second gig is big enough. It is done in a transparent manner by both. Some employers even take a stake in the start-up.

7. **A start-up is born**: Many start-ups are born when colleagues pick up the ropes during their time as employees. Sachin and Binny Bansal worked at Amazon before launching Flipkart. That is when they understood how to build a scalable e-commerce start-up. Film actors like Naseeruddin Shah, Ratna Pathak Shah, Pankaj Kapoor etc. play to packed auditoriums and multiplexes alike as they juggle theatre and cinema.

8. **Some professions have it easier**: Software developers often take up small projects that last a few days or even a few months and make some money on the side. Working on these projects is a great way to keep their skills updated. The Great Resignation has resulted in several employers being forced to work with freelancers and gig workers. Many more people can use these projects to build a financial cushion before they switch to Career 2.0.

The line between a job and moonlighting is getting blurred

As previously discussed, I wasn't quite prepared for how employers would respond to the idea of moonlighting.

Moonlighting to build up a skill seems to be socially acceptable but doing it to earn more seems to be frowned upon.

Software giant Oracle has created more than one job opportunity for its employees, who are encouraged to take up multiple projects within the organization. They call it 'ethical moonlighting'.

Besides, for external opportunities, Oracle uses the following criteria to evaluate the side gig and give it a stamp of formal approval. The company asks four questions:

- Is there a financial implication for the employer or employee? How will it be accounted for?
- Is the intellectual property of the firm being used? If there is intellectual property being created with the side gig, who owns it?
- Does the moonlighting project dilute the employer's competitive edge?
- Are office resources being used and is there anything that may harm the employer's interests? Do not use the office laptop or Internet connection to do any moonlighting projects is a standard piece of advice given.

Adobe offers four weeks of paid leave to employees with five years of service to the company so they can 'plan their dream vacation' or 'finally write that novel'. Google started a fellowship programme that allowed employees to spend up to six months working for non-profits on special projects.

Case: Tangelo ice creams after the end of Career 1.0

Pawan Malhotra is seventy-three and retired from his corporate career. His traditional corporate career followed the path that many MBAs have trodden. He worked at Dunlop, Unilever, PepsiCo, Al Futtaim, and ONDP and finally retired as the CEO and MD of Mahindra Lifespaces. He lived across India, the United Arab Emirates and Oman following his corporate jobs.

The one thing he was curious about all his life, ever since he was a little boy, was to learn how ice cream and dessert were made across the world. He travelled all over the world during his career and in every corner of India and every part of the world, the one thing he made sure he sampled was the local ice cream and dessert.

Pawan is the type of person who likes to keep busy and connect with people and the world around him.

'I started making ice cream on the weekends after the Haagen Dazs in Oman closed down and there was no other good ice cream. Yes, my standards are high! Gourmet ice cream is my passion. My first attempts were like science experiments, but trial and error, a training course in Italy and persistence finally led to an ice cream that friends in Oman loved.

'When I moved to Gurugram upon retiring, I had a professional ice cream kitchen built in the basement of my home, allowing me to pursue my hobby of making ice cream. In fact, we had moved so much over the years we had to pick a city to retire in. We chose Gurgaon so we could build a bungalow with my ice cream kitchen in it.

'My wife and I also planted a kitchen garden with fruit and vegetables not easily available in India. I've found that once you start something, consistent little steps make it grow even if that was not your intention when you started out. So, our kitchen garden eventually provided fruit for my ice cream.

'My ice cream became completely natural with real ingredients—nothing artificial and no preservatives. I often got requests for ice cream from people who were diabetic, weight-conscious, lactose intolerant or with other dietary restrictions. So, the ice cream is sugar-free, low calorie and vegan as well.'

It is now a brand called Tangelo with outlets at Select Citywalk Mall in Delhi, One Horizon in Gurgaon, Kidzania in Noida as well as the Delhi Golf Club and Delhi Gymkhana. It's definitely not a hobby anymore!

9

Career 3.0

Our education and our social systems encourage people to focus on learning just one thing at a time. The person who studies science is expected to be uninterested in history or music. The coder is expected to be less proficient in languages. When we see someone who is interested in multiple areas beyond academics and school texts, teachers and parents see it as a distraction.

Consumers do not think of silos. Neither do our colleagues. It is no surprise that individual contributors who excel at their work flounder and fail as people managers. After being unidimensional for twenty years, suddenly they have to appreciate others' emotions, aspirations and dreams.

Case: Aditya Ghosh

Aditya Ghosh was working in a law firm where InterGlobe Enterprise was his client. They invited him to join the airline when he was barely twenty-seven. Two years later, he wrote the application for the airline's licence. Under his leadership, IndiGo became the most successful Indian airline, commanding a 40 per cent market share.

He ran the company for a decade until he quit in 2018. During his tenure, he built a culture where an employee's achievements outside of work were also recognized. The IndiGo pilot who had joined the masterchef contest was applauded, the flight attendant who pursued fencing appeared on the cover of the inflight magazine and so on. 'I went on to create programmes where we would celebrate such colleagues because they have shown the ability to work with diverse groups of people from pilots and flight attendants to chefs and sportspeople,' he says.

Aditya attributes this perspective to the way his parents raised him. In school, he was a debater who was equally passionate about science, history and music. He chose to study science in school but loved studying history and languages too. As a business leader, he was able to learn from experts like the head of engineering or the head of inflight service where he would be an apprentice and follow instructions. 'Whether it is the coach who's teaching me tennis or horse riding and golf, I always call them "sir" because it reminds me that I am a student,' recalls Aditya.

Whether at Indigo or later, Aditya created a portfolio of work that had a mix of operational, strategic growth and scaling up of businesses as well as social impact projects.

In addition, he made time to learn how to ski and ride horses, tried to learn to play the piano (which he failed at, he confesses) and continued writing columns or speaking at conferences. Aditya Ghosh describes himself as an entrepreneur, the founder of Homage and the co-founder of the rapidly growing airlines called Akasa Air.

'I experienced three lifetimes in three careers'

I spoke to several people in the process of writing this book. It only reinforced my belief that our career is a journey through life. This journey is unique to the individual. No matter how much we benchmark somebody, our career path will always be unique. No one else will experience the same choices. Even identical twins experience different levels of success and happiness during different moments in life.

Each one of the people that I spoke to told me that their actual path had turned out to be completely different from what they had anticipated at the start of their careers.

S.M. (name withheld on request) is the CEO of a very successful organization. In the past, he has been the head of two of India's biggest consulting firms. I asked him what he considered the reason for his success.

'I don't feel that I am successful. I have been lucky at times and very unlucky at times,' he said, with a hint of sadness in his voice. 'You could say that I have experienced three different lifetimes in one.'

I did not want to interrupt his thoughts and let him continue.

'I wanted to study economics just as my parents had. My grandfather wanted me to be an engineer. I did not like maths, and you could say that I was ill-placed to be successful as an engineer. By a strange quirk of fate, I ended up studying at an engineering college. To avoid working as an engineer, I went to a business school and completed my MBA. My first job was in sales. For some years, I stayed in the organization that I had joined through the campus placement, without ever thinking about a change of jobs. That was my first life. I had no complaints and felt adequately rewarded, thanks to all the promotions and increments that I received.'

He sipped his coffee and continued, 'Even as a child I was very strongly inclined towards spiritual matters. At the age of twenty-nine, I decided to quit the corporate world and join a monastery to become a monk. I wore a white kurta and dhoti and walked barefoot as I travelled the length and breadth of India with my spiritual master. I read the scriptures and built the membership of the sect I was a part of. Being an engineer and MBA helped me bring a number of skills to the monastery. During the eight years I spent at the monastery, never for a minute did I think that I would do something else. When my spiritual master called me one day, I was completely unprepared for what was to follow. I presumed it would be all about serving at the new hospital we were building. I was excited about learning new skills and being able to serve in a different capacity.'

'What was the meeting about?'

'My spiritual master called me and said that it was time for me to leave this world and continue my quest in the corporate world. I was confused. I had left the business world to be part of the spiritual organization and was prepared to serve it for the rest of my life. As I stepped outside the door of the monastery, I realized I was thirty-seven years old and utterly unprepared to re-enter a world that had changed so drastically in those eight years. I felt like Rip Van Winkle. My second life had ended, and I did not know how to get started with the third act. I had left the corporate world when it had been operating with landlines and typewriters and I was unprepared for a world which had been taken over by computers and automation. I applied for a series of jobs and was not even called for an interview.'

He walked up to the window and looked out. I suspect this bit was not easy for him to talk about.

'I met a few of my classmates from business school and felt that they were light years ahead of me. I could not even communicate confidently with them. It was as if the eight years in the monastery had wiped out everything that I had learned in college. A cousin suggested that I should work with a search firm and look for a job. The search firms had no interest in talking to somebody like me who had quit a corporate career to become a monk and now wanted to get back to join the rat race again. I met a classmate at a headhunter's office. He was going to start his own firm and decided to take a chance on me. He gave me a break and a chance to rebuild my life.'

After spending a decade at his friend's firm, S.M. rediscovered his confidence. When his friend decided to shut down the firm, S.M. had no problem finding another job. He got the opportunity to lead a division at one of the big four accounting firms. In the last few years, he has been invited to be the CEO of a global consulting giant and a start-up that has since become a unicorn, thanks to his Midas touch.

'It is possible to reinvent yourself at any age,' said S.M., when I asked him about the lessons, he had learned on his career journey. 'It is not just about skills and competencies. People play a very large role. At every stage of your career, someone has to take a chance and believe that you can do a job that you have never done before. Finding such a person is a matter of luck, wouldn't you say that?'

Forces shaping the Career 3.0 archetype

As the nature of work is evolving, so are the career archetypes. Career 1.0 and Career 2.0 are giving way to Career 3.0. Career 1.0 can be described as a tunnel with three stages: learn, earn and retire. Career 2.0 is like a fork in the road, with side gigs carried out after office hours in stealth mode. Once the side hustle starts generating funds, it leaves open the possibility of becoming the main career path.

To visualize Career 3.0, think of it as a pizza in which each slice is a skill. The skill can be based on your deep domain knowledge, your emotional intelligence, creative thinking etc. The key to success in Career 3.0 is to develop a range of skills and keep creating combinations of the skills that are valued in the marketplace. Another way to think of the pizza is look at those slices as the percentage of time spent on each distinct activity.

Authors Ravin Jesuthasan and John W. Boudreau describe the coming few years as a time when organizations will have to rethink the operating system around work and workers. Automation and AI will augment the work of the employees. In their book *Work Without Jobs,* they describe a future where workers will advance their careers through their skills and capabilities—not through seniority.

By 2025, eighty-five million jobs may be displaced by a shift in the division of labour between humans and machines. At the same time, ninety-seven million new roles will emerge that need humans, machines, and algorithms to work in tandem.

1. A longer lifespan means having to work more years

When the pandemic struck, it triggered a race to create a vaccine against a new virus that was a stranger to the world before 2020. Improved healthcare, sanitation, immunizations, access to clean running water, and better nutrition are all combining to create greater life expectancy. In 1950, the average life expectancy in India was thirty-two years, as compared to sixty-eight years in the US. In 2020, the average life expectancy in India was more than seventy years while the US now has a life expectancy of seventy-nine years.

As of 2016, children born in the West have a fifty per cent chance of living to age 105, says Lynda Gratton in her book *The 100-Year Life.* According to mortality.org, the oldest age at which fifty per cent of the babies born in 2007 are predicted to be still alive for the US, Italy, France and Canada is 104. That age is 103 for the UK, 102 for Germany and 107 for Japan.

Think about what it means to live to be 100 years old. Someone who enters the workforce at the age of twenty may well have to work into their eighties or nineties. Lifetime employment has been slowly replaced by the need to have lifetime relevance and employability. In the US, 3.2 per cent of workers who retired in 2021 had rejoined the workforce by late 2022—about 1.7 million people.[*]

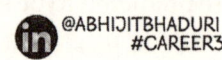

[*] Louis, Serah, '"There Is No More Retirement": Runaway Prices Are Pushing Seniors Back to Work as the Future of Social Security Remains "under Threat"', Yahoo, 1 November 2022, https://finance.yahoo.com/news/no-more-retirement-runaway-prices-140000229.html, accessed on 16 July 2023.

2. Older workers are 'unretiring'

With the pandemic under control, a lot of older workers feel more secure coming back to the workplace. In some cases, the rising inflation has eaten into their retirement savings, and it is forcing them to replenish their bank accounts. In some sectors such as hospitality, retail and leisure, the wage rates have climbed up significantly and are attractive enough to tempt some people to rejoin the workforce.

The longevity of the human population affects the way we view career trajectories. When I was growing up, it was common for my friends to say, 'I will make my millions by the time I'm thirty, and then just chill.' Even after people hit their financial goals, they continue to work for a variety of reasons. Staying mentally alert and healthy is an important benefit of continuing to work for as many years as possible. The demands of a routine, following deadlines, meeting colleagues and the social aspects of work have a powerful impact on our mental health.

DJ Sumirock

Sumiko Iwamuro, who was born in Japan in 1935, holds the world record for being the oldest professional club disc jockey (DJ). She spent most of her life working in a restaurant. She went to a school for DJing and learnt how to mix music when she was seventy-seven years old, after her husband passed away. She is now known as DJ Sumirock. By day, this Japanese woman runs a Chinese restaurant with her brother and by night, she DJs at a club in Tokyo. She proves that age is no bar to chasing a dream.

Living longer changes how we work. The industry where we work is more likely to be affected by internal or external forces over a few decades. The probability of a new manager's view about our work and capabilities impacting us increases with every passing year. Longevity affects how many years we live after our sources of income dry up. When we live longer, many of the things that were large problems to solve even a few decades back suddenly become easier as innovations happen.

Sometimes it is about creating a second career or a 'portfolio career' as Reid Hoffman, the co-founder of LinkedIn, puts it. He describes his career as having two phases: the first is a hyper-focused phase where he was an employee at Fujitsu and then at Apple. During this phase, he built deep skills in product design and user experience design. It also gave him first-hand experience of how to run a tech company. Then came the phase when Reid was building LinkedIn, investing in other tech companies, doing charity work, authoring books and hosting multiple podcasts.[*]

As I studied the career paths of several such people, I found that it is a lot like learning to juggle first with two objects and getting good at it, before adding a third and fourth object to juggle. A long life is going to force many people to keep reinventing themselves. If human beings are living longer, the lifespan of large corporations is shrinking at a steady pace.

---

[*] 'The Startup of You Podcast', LinkedIn, n.d., https://podcasts.apple.com/us/podcast/the-startup-of-you-podcast/id1611250417, accessed on 16 July 2023.

3. Most businesses do not last as long anymore

Human longevity comes with another challenge. There are not enough employers who can outlive human beings, who are living longer. The average age of a company listed on S&P 500 has fallen from almost sixty years in the 1950s to less than twenty years currently.[*]

According to the US Bureau of Labor Statistics, 20 per cent of all businesses last less than two years. Forty-five per cent of businesses collapse within the first five years and only 15 per cent of businesses make it past fifteen years.

The notion of someone experiencing the stability and predictability of a secure job is becoming a thing of the past. Even the jobs in the government, once seen as the benchmark of stable employment, are coming under pressure. Different parts of the government's business are being outsourced to private players. The Indian Railways outsourced the operation and maintenance of railway stations to companies outside state control for fifteen years with the aim of improving customer experience. Stations will be handed over to the state-run Indian Railways Station Development Corporation which will subsequently invite bids from private companies to operate and maintain these stations.

In my book *Dreamers and Unicorns*, I described 'Dreamers' as the first phase in which a company gets

---

[*] Sheetz, Michael, 'Technology Killing off Corporate America: Average Life Span of Companies under 20 Years', CNBC, 24 August 2017, https://www.cnbc.com/2017/08/24/technology-killing-off-corporations-average-lifespan-of-company-under-20-years.html, accessed on 16 July 2023.

formed and tries to discover its product market fit. This is the phase when it needs to raise funds, hire employees and show to the investors that it has a practical business model. The term 'Unicorn' is used to describe the second phase of growth where a firm scales up and expands its geographic footprint. This is the phase of hyper growth and the most difficult to manage.

When a start-up firm seeks to borrow money from investors, the founders must convince the investors about the feasibility of its scale-up plans. Scaling up from a small firm run by a handful of people means being able to build the organization that can support this rapid growth phase. An increase in complexity and geographic presence is directly visible. Running the business in a scalable manner means standardizing various parts of the process.

Turning a Unicorn into a 'Market Shaper' involves building global presence and brand recognition. In this journey, the leader's vision attracts the talent that is needed, but it is ultimately the organization's culture which keeps the talent. This phase of hyper growth is also when the leaders find it hard to spend time building the talent strategy or cultural norms.

4. The half-life of most skills is dropping

Your mobile phone continuously displays how much battery life is left before it goes dead. Imagine seeing the same information for your skills. The value of a skill is measured in 'half-life'. The value of a skill drops over time because of changes in technology, automation or dropping demand for the skill. When a skill is only half as valuable, that is called its half-life. In 2017, the World Economic Forum had estimated the half-life of a skill to be five years.[*] The half-life of most technical skills is around two years. The half-life of a skill like driving may be more in a country like India because traffic is often chaotic. That is why self-driving cars will take longer to appear on Indian streets.

Already AI is able to accurately detect cancer better than a doctor. The software got it right in 95 per cent of images of cancerous moles and benign spots, whereas a team of fifty-eight dermatologists was accurate 87 per cent of the time. There are many firms like Wealthfront, SoFi, Fidelity, etc. that offer robot investing services, also known as robo-advisors. These firms use algorithms to manage investment portfolios for their clients. The voices of the late Anthony Bourdain and the late Andy Warhol have both been recreated for recent documentaries by AI.

The market pays for the skills that it needs. These are the marketable skills that determine employability. Niche skills are the ones that are not yet being taught in a structured way by skill providers, like a school or college. A niche skill is learnt through trial and error from a bunch of explorers trying to make sense of things. People who build niche skills are much sought after by businesses that are also early adopters. These skills often have evangelists who are self-taught. The demand for niche skills always outstrips

[*] Anon, 'Skill, Re-Skill and Re-Skill Again. How to Keep up with the Future of Work', World Economic Forum, 6 February 2020, https://www.weforum.org/agenda/2017/07/skill-reskill-prepare-for-future-of-work/, accessed on 4 August 2023.

the supply, giving people with those skills tremendous bargaining power with employers.

The market is continuously looking for niche skills in every sector because that is what gives a head start to the businesses. When people discover the premium that the market offers for these skills, they will want to learn the skill. This demand is met by an increasing number of skill providers. What was once a niche skill becoming more commonplace. The demand for the skill then matches its supply and turns it into a marketable skill. Marketable skills get monetized very easily. When employers ask for a degree or any other academic qualification before they hire someone, it is because the degree serves as a proxy for a marketable skill. Having marketable skills helps people get paid on a par with everyone who has that skill. For instance, most coders get paid at market rates.

Some skills are common to everyone in the workplace. We stop mentioning them in our CVs. They get labelled as commodity skills. Commodity skills are those which many people possess but they do not get monetized. Some of us may recall that people used to list 'proficiency in Word, Excel and PowerPoint' on their CVs. Today, it is not a differentiator in the marketplace. Mentioning these skills on your CV does not get you noticed by any recruiter because these are now commoditized. Not having this skill is a disadvantage but having the skill is not a differentiator in the job market.

The skills that are most sought after in the marketplace are the ones where demand outstrips supply. These are the niche skills that are hard to teach, or not enough institutions teach them, or the technology is still evolving. Early adopters are the ones who have the skills that the employers are desperate to hire for. These skills are often needed for technology that is still nascent. For instance, digital mapping is an interdisciplinary study that brings together geography, computer science, design and other fields to create new and useful ways to organize our world. From Google Maps to Homeland Security, digital mapping is central, using data to find patterns and locate threats.

People with niche skills are specialists who usually combine multiple disciplines to build their skills. Ethical hacking and psychometrics are both examples of niche skills.

What is a niche skill today will become a marketable skill once educational institutions start churning out more people with that skill. Skill combinations also create unique capabilities. A strong domain knowledge combined with social media skills plus the ability to build a community and the ability to monetize it can create a niche in the job market.

While education and employability have enjoyed close ties historically, that is changing. The jobs that asked for a bachelor's degree now ask for a master's. This is described as degree inflation.

Blue-collar, white-collar and eventually no-collar workforce

Case: Maqbool Fida Husain

Maqbool Fida Husain (1915–2011) was an Indian artist known for executing bold, vibrantly coloured narrative paintings in a modified Cubist style. He was one of the most celebrated and internationally recognized Indian artists of the twentieth century. F.N. Souza, who founded the Progressive Artists' Group in 1947, once declared that the secret of Husain's success was '40 per cent your beard, 30 per cent your personality, 20 per cent your friends, and 10 per cent maybe your talent!'

'I don't need any degree because of this brush in my hand,' Husain recalled telling his family upon finishing high school. 'If nothing happens, I'll whitewash the walls.'

Incarnations: A History of India in 50 Lives written by historian Sunil Khilnani has an insightful paragraph on Husain: 'He began his career as a professional artist in Bombay, where he painted garish Bollywood film hoardings for a pittance. Typically working outdoors, sometimes between monsoon downpours, he mastered with confident strokes a scale and sense of proportion that other artists working on large canvases would have required detailed sketches and grids to pull off. Years later, when extremist vandals ransacked his home, destroying paintings worth millions on the market, he accepted it with equanimity: 'I know how it is to work so hard on a hoarding that is put up for only a couple of weeks, and then destroyed. Isn't it funny?'

Husain started painting miniatures in 1941 to decorate nurseries. He also designed furniture. It was his ability to create his signature style and the ease with which he socialized that made him irresistible to prime ministers, film stars and common art lovers alike. Husain symbolized the transition from blue-collar to white-collar and eventually the no-collar workforce. He was immune to praise and criticism and walked his path alone.

One of the most important lessons that we can learn from creators is not to get attached to our own creations. Husain certainly embodied that philosophy.

Case: From corn farmer to digital entrepreneur

Ganesh Nazirkar is a twenty-seven-year-old grape farmer. He knows what matters to his community of farmers. For instance, when he realized that a lot of the farmers from his region were growing the wrong variety of corn seed depending on soil and water conditions, he started organizing various innovation festivals to educate them on the various technological solutions that could bring about a better harvest.

His events are funded by various companies who want to reach farmers and local traders. He uses social media, especially WhatsApp and Instagram videos, to influence farmers in the region, and also promotes new agritech products and solutions on various channels. Such change makers from local communities, who are empathetic and drive the community forward, are great examples of digital economy leaders in their own right.

Ganesh was part of a two-month programme offered by ChanceLabs. The Digital Leadership programme gave him an opportunity to further his true potential and also to be able to afford a comfortable lifestyle with the extra earnings. His exposure to structured learnings around entrepreneurship and digital media has strengthened his role as an influencer in his community. Ganesh is also actively trying to create and manage a network of more such digital champions. He will also act as a role model and mentor for others who want to ride the opportunities in the digital economy. He takes pride in describing himself today as a farmer who is also a small business owner.

Degree Inflation—when degrees lose their market value

If the job does not require a post-graduate degree, should you hire a candidate who has a post-graduate degree? If a candidate with a PhD has willingly applied to do a job that needs only a grade five education, should you reject that candidate?

That is the kind of scenario that plays out repeatedly in many cases. When the Uttar Pradesh police department advertised for sixty-two positions of messengers, they received applications from 3,700 PhDs, 28,000 post-graduates and 50,000 graduates for a job that barely needs literacy. The job simply expected the candidate to have a fifth-grade school education and know how to ride a cycle.[*]

In 2015, 67 per cent of production supervisor job postings asked for a college degree. Only 16 per cent of employed production supervisors had this qualification. That raises the cost of hire and the time to hire increases. Degree Inflation is a killer when it comes to the bottom line.

Tech firms like Apple, IBM, Amazon and a few others like EY have stripped off the requirement

[*] Online, Et, 'Over 93,000 Candidates, Including 3,700 PhD Holders Apply for Peon Job in UP', *Economic Times*, *30 August 2018,* https://economictimes.indiatimes.com/ news/politics-and-nation/over-93000-candidates-including-3700-phd-holders-apply-for-peon-job-in-up/articleshow/65604396.cms, accessed 4 August 2023.

for degrees. Some others like Hilton Hotels have also moved in this direction. Employers are moving in tentatively. If a job does not need a degree while entering, will it become a limitation for the employee to get a promotion at a later point, they wonder.

Microsoft has been recruiting, developing and upskilling unconventional talent for employability into the technology industry worldwide through its LEAP programme since 2015. In Lagos, Nigeria, the programme attracts talent looking to build careers as data analysts. In Australia and New Zealand, cloud solutions architects are groomed through the LEAP programme. Whether it's a stay-at-home parent interested in re-entering the workforce or someone who is ready for a 'second act', the LEAP programme celebrates learners who want to build a career in tech but may not have a computer science degree. Learning agility, and not the degree, matters.

Does the Career 3.0 archetype apply to people who are employed in a corporation and have no desire to voluntarily start anything on their own? It is possible to have a Career 3.0 mindset even for an employee. An employee who has built strong skills by working in running the supply chain in different countries, is good at leading teams and has strong business acumen is more valuable than most others.

It is the portfolio of skills that drives Career 3.0

If you are employed, take these two tests to check your readiness for Career 2.0 or Career 3.0

These are the two tests you can take.

1. The twelve-month experiment:

Will there be a need to compromise on your lifestyle if you take your side hustle and make it your main source of income? Changing career tracks means you will quit your job and switch to the uncertainty and excitement that come from being a freelancer. There is only one way to figure that out. You have to spend twelve months living on just the money that you make from your side hustle. You have to spend the year without touching the salary that you get from your employer. That includes spending money on eating out as often as you normally do, taking vacations as you normally do or spending money on necessities (e.g., healthcare expenses) and luxuries as you are used to. If you are able to do it, you are ready for Career 3.0, or at least Career 2.0.

2. Operating autonomously:

Being an employee often does not offer people the ability to be accountable for their decisions. As an entrepreneur, you will have to operate autonomously. This is a very different experience as compared to being an employee. You have to own the consequences of every decision that you take whether it is minor or major. A freelancer once told me, 'When I had to decide which laptop to buy, it was a strange feeling. As an employee, it is the IT department that decides which laptop to buy. If something does not work, someone from the IT team will repair it. I realized that day, I am the chief information officer and the chief financial officer, and the purchase department all rolled into one! If something goes wrong, it is my decision.'

You can build this attitude of operating autonomously while still being at a desk job. Here are some things you can do to get started:

- Do five things which your boss has not put into the current year's objectives.
- Create five services that can benefit your current employer.
- Think of a pain point in your current organization. (Figure out a way to solve it. Remember, you have to do all this without taking on extra resources. That is a great way to experience what entrepreneurs go through every day.)

As an employee, you don't do anything which doesn't have a return on investment (ROI)—you get a promotion or bonus or incentive or at least somebody gives you a thank you note or something. When you do gig work, you must do a number of things which have no immediate ROI. You do it because you enjoy doing it.

Case: From engineering to consulting, then poaching and coaching

Deepak Jayaraman is an executive coach and the CEO of Transition Insight, where he works with successful senior executives and helps them play to their unique potential by working with them closely during phases of high stakes transition. He is also the host of a very popular podcast *Play to Potential* where he talks to leaders and thinkers to explore how they handle leadership moments, transitions and careers. I will let Deepak describe his career path that is full of choices, transitions and uncertainties—as all career paths are. Being an engineer–MBA, how did he become a podcaster or a coach or a keynote speaker? Let us find out.

Phase 1—Career 1.0

'My journey, till I was thirty-three, could be characterized as that of an aspiring middle-class Indian who put his blinkers on and worked hard to achieve some sort of escape velocity in order to try and break through the gravitational forces of middle class living in Chennai where I went to school.

'I then studied at IIT Madras, IIMA and at London Business School. I started working at KPMG in London and moved to McKinsey, New Jersey, as a consultant. My primary focus was on earning money and maximizing financial outcomes, given the skills and capabilities I had.

'In late 2008 and early 2009, all that changed with one phone call. My father was diagnosed with stage four colon cancer. I came back to India with McKinsey to take care of his treatment. He passed away in six months, but I was grateful for the opportunity to spend time with him.

'It was a life-changing moment that led me to understand what energized me (which turned out to be slightly different from the areas where I was skilled). I had always told myself that I was this 'Quant guy' who was good at problem solving but I felt that I got my energy from solving complex people-related problems.

Phase 2—Picking the right exit of the motorway

It gave me a sense of what mattered in life. A nudge from a mentor at McKinsey (Ramesh Mangaleswaran) got me to Egon Zehnder where I got an opportunity to work with clients on CEO, CXO and board searches. While it was directionally the right step from McKinsey, I felt three disconnects at that stage:

- The bulk of the time was spent in evaluative conversations which I found to be draining; I felt I got my energy from enabling conversations.
- Someone else was setting the pace of the treadmill of my life (demands of partnership).

I was left with little bandwidth to pursue some of my creative interests (I used to enjoy playing the guitar, juggling balls, and creating content as a hobby).

Ongoing pursuit of Ikigai

I have now been doing two things since 2016.

- Firstly, I work as an executive coach/sounding board to CEOs, promoters, partners and investors. This requires me to understand their personal and professional world deeply and to be of value to them in their growth journey. They also rope me in on some of the key choices they have to make.

- Secondly, I curate the Play to Potential podcast (www. playtopotential.com) where I speak to thinkers and leaders from different walks of life on leadership, transitions and careers.

The podcast works primarily as my Learning and Development function. Here is a space where I get to sharpen my saw over the long term in the space where I want to build my advisory practice. Over time, it has also led to people building trust in me and the work I do. Most importantly, it gives people an opportunity to discern my WHY. It has slowly started playing the role of a content marketing function and has helped me move from being sales led (Push) to being marketing led (Pull). The podcast has also given me an opportunity to be of value in some of the social media networks and to say something of meaning and substance (rather than forwarding pieces created by others).

Over the last few years, I am also taking my baby steps in the world of social change (giving time, money and knowledge). I am a member of Social Venture Partners, a group of philanthropists. Through this group, I got a chance to interact with Vinay Hebbar, who is with Harvard Business Publishing. He has been kind enough to be on the advisory board of the podcast. I also got a chance to hire a couple of individuals who hail from underprivileged backgrounds. They now work as editor and social media manager at the podcast respectively. It brings greater meaning to the work I do.

My current commercial model consists of two legs (with an emerging third and fourth leg):

o *Current*

- Advisory income from one-on-one coaching and sounding board advisory with leaders.
- Keynote speeches with some corporates where I share some of my learnings from the Play to Potential podcast.

o *Emerging*

- After about six years of curating the podcast, I am on the cusp of introducing a freemium model that would put some of the content at the podcast behind a paywall.
- I also plan to launch a community of sorts (inspired by an organization like YPO)* where I get to work with like-minded leaders.
- I plan to write a book (or a series) in the near future where I will capture some of the reflections from my journey, coaching work and the podcast.

I have found it useful to think about the current phase of my life as a flywheel where I think about each decision and see if it adds to the flywheel or not. As an independent producer, I get to have control over the pace of the flywheel

---

* Young Presidents' Organization, a global leadership community of extraordinary chief executives.

and operate it a bit like a thermostat. Whenever it starts spinning too fast, I decide to trip the supply (by saying no to things or being extremely selective) and slow it down. I have begun to value direction more than distance in this phase of my life where I am trying to be mindful of how much time I spend at work vis-a-vis other areas of my life.

Career 3.0 is an archetype built around a mindset

Can you learn what you do not know yet?

Ninety billion nerve cells, also known as neurons, make up a person's brain. That is more than ten times the number of human beings on planet earth. It is no surprise that the brain is one of the most complicated organs we have. The neurons are connected to each other through synapses. This is where a signal is sent from one cell to another and is translated into a chemical message. These neurotransmitters hold many of the unsolved mysteries that lie behind our capabilities. More than 100 neurotransmitters have been discovered but there are many more we do not know enough about. One of the big mysteries we are discovering is that we are all capable of learning new skills continuously. That our brain has the capacity to expand what it can do. This is the science of neuroplasticity. When we learn something new, it is the equivalent of creating a small pathway between two neurons. When we try doing something over and over again, the pathway becomes more prominent and easily accessible.

Research findings on neuroplasticity of the brain encourage people to learn things as opportunities come up.

The opportunities may be around us, but do we have the mindset that we need to thrive? Your mindset is a set of beliefs that shape how you make sense of the world and yourself. It influences how you think, feel, and behave in any given situation.

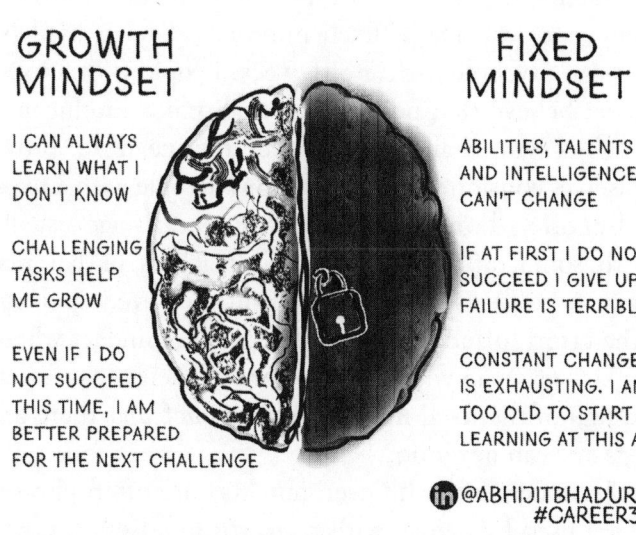

GROWTH MINDSET

I CAN ALWAYS LEARN WHAT I DON'T KNOW

CHALLENGING TASKS HELP ME GROW

EVEN IF I DO NOT SUCCEED THIS TIME, I AM BETTER PREPARED FOR THE NEXT CHALLENGE

FIXED MINDSET

ABILITIES, TALENTS AND INTELLIGENCE CAN'T CHANGE

IF AT FIRST I DO NOT SUCCEED I GIVE UP. FAILURE IS TERRIBLE.

CONSTANT CHANGE IS EXHAUSTING. I AM TOO OLD TO START LEARNING AT THIS AGE

@ABHIJITBHADURI
#CAREER3

Fixed mindset or growth mindset?

Which of these statements do you agree with?

1. We are born with a certain talent and that cannot be changed.
2. Even if I don't know something, I can learn it.
3. A failure is a sign that we have reached the limit of our capability.

4. A failure is a way of learning something.
5. I am good at a few things and terrible at some other things.
6. I am good at what I have worked at. I will get better at whatever I continue working at.

The statements with the odd numbers reflect the beliefs of someone who has a 'fixed mindset'—a term used by American psychologist Carol Dweck. People with a fixed mindset believe that neither personality nor intelligence are subject to change. They feel the need to prove themselves constantly in all situations. People with a fixed mindset often develop this outlook at an early age, usually due to some influence from their teachers or parents. Parents who focus only on the results achieved, and not on the effort, often unknowingly create a mindset where their kids grow up with fixed notions of their capabilities. One sign of the fixed mindset is the belief that there are things one can never do.

The statements with even numbers are often phrases that are used by people with a growth mindset, as Carol Dweck would say.

People with a growth mindset believe that intelligence and talents can be developed over time. It is possible to change your personality traits and grow your abilities continuously. People with a growth mindset love to learn and continue to build on their portfolio of skills.

In a world where there is constant change, being able to adapt to changes, and trying to learn what one has not been taught is an important by-product of someone who has a growth mindset.

Follow creators to understand how Career 3.0 works

Creators have had to work outside the traditional employment models. The career track of a musician or actor does not follow the norms of the stable Career 1.0 model. They have to juggle multiple opportunities. It is very common for the theatre actor to do a role in a movie or to be the host of a radio show. A movie star has to deal with the fame and attention that come with a box office hit as well as the experience of getting ignored by fans when a film flops. Being a good actor is necessary but not sufficient. Being unable to handle a continuous flow of transitions and change of fame and fortunes causes people to quit.

The creator economy is thriving. Some YouTubers are richer than CEOs. Have you heard of Ajey Nagar? Maybe you should look him up on YouTube where he is known as CarryMinati. This twenty-four-year-old Indian YouTuber has over 39.7 million subscribers and is estimated to be worth close to $10 million. All this from making videos where he is roasting and dissing others. Nagar was named the 10th Next Generation Leaders 2019 by *Time* magazine in 2019. This is an annual list of ten young people who build innovative careers. He was named one of Forbes' 30 Under 30 Asia in April 2020.*

Bhuvan Bam's comedy channel BB ki Vines has over 26.3 million subscribers. He is not just a comedian but also

---

* Desk, Sk, 'How Much Is CarryMinati's Net Worth as of 2022?', Sports Keeda, 19 October 2022, https://wiki.sportskeeda.com/ youtube/what-is-carryminati-net-worth, accessed on 4 July 2023.

a writer, singer and songwriter. He used to be a musician in Moti Mahal, Saket in New Delhi and was paid Rs 5000 (approx $60) per gig. He sang ghazals and popular songs of Mohammed Rafi, Kishore Kumar and Hemant Kumar.

Starting his YouTube channel was a game changer for him. He created several unique characters for his sketches including the very popular Titu Mama. Bhuvan Bam has a net worth of around $15 million, which is around Rs 122 crore. His net worth stems from his brand and endorsement deals, as well as his web series, movie roles and YouTube revenue from videos.

Vidya Vox aka Vidya Iyer is an Indian-origin YouTuber and singer. She started her channel in 2015 and has over seven million subscribers and has a net worth of about $1.3 million.* The Creator Economy is creating the biggest opportunities ever and people across age groups are all ready to be 'employed' by viewers.

Blogger, podcaster, professional poker player, journalist, and online writing coach Amit Varma spoke to me about the forces that are shaping the creator economy.

1. **Ownership of the means of production**: The average smartphone camera plus access to Instagram can turn any budding photographer into a star. A few years back, softwares like DaVinci Resolve (used for

---

* DNA Web Team, 'Meet Vidya Vox, One of India's Richest Female YouTubers, Her Net Worth Is', DNA India, 22 July 2023. https://www.dnaindia.com/business/report-meet-vidya-vox-one-of-india-s-richest-female-youtubers-her-net-worth-is-3052863, accessed on 4 August 2023.

colour grading) cost up to $8,00,000 and needed a high-powered computer to run it. It was used only by Hollywood movie studios. Today, anyone can download a free version of the software and get started. There is a free tutorial on YouTube that can teach you the basics.

2. **No gatekeepers between the creator and the reader**: In the past, the editors of newspapers and magazines would traditionally decide which article or post would get printed. No more. The Internet has changed that. Writers can publish their own novels even if no publishing house wants to sign them on. Earlier, Bollywood directors and writers would decide which actor would play the lead. A handful of singers, writers, sound engineers and cameramen ruled the roost. YouTube democratized the creation of content and made it possible for anyone to make a film on a mobile phone and post it for the world to see. YouTube is the fourth-largest seller of digital ads after its parent company, Alphabet, Facebook, and Amazon, as per *Fortune*. There are no barriers to entry—only talent.

3. **No limitations and restrictions on word count or time**: A newspaper column had to be around 700 to 1000 words. Film songs in Bollywood were under four minutes. To be featured on a vinyl record, the classical musician had to carefully fit their composition into the time allocated by the album producer. But a blogger can decide to write a 100-word post or a 1,00,000-word post. The choice is theirs. It promotes the opportunity to be unrestrained when it comes to ideas and creativity. Amit Varma's podcast *The Seen*

and the Unseen is one of the most popular podcasts in India. His episodes last approximately four to eight *hours!* These are conversations on economics, politics and literature. It is a free-flowing conversation that goes down various topics and subtopics. 'I would have never been able to produce a five-hour long podcast if I depended on mainstream media houses,' he says.

4. **A direct connection with the audience:** When I write a post on LinkedIn, the subscribers respond back with comments, suggestions and even fact-checks. The relationship between the writer and the reader is intimate. Kaushiki Chakraborty is a classical singer whose fans send her their own practice videos. Kaushiki shares her feedback for them to build on. The silver screen hero of the yesteryears was inaccessible. Today's creators are in constant conversation with their audience. It is this two-way conversation that builds the fan base. It is a relationship that is dependent on building trust. Every influencer is in the business of trust. When they recommend or endorse a product, their fans buy the product. Credibility and consistency are the foundation of every creator.

5. **A thousand true fans are all that you need:** Kevin Kelly had famously predicted that a thousand true fans who would pay $100 annually could give a creator an annual income of $1,00,000. Some writers like Li Jin show that a 100 superfans paying $1,000 (or its equivalent) every year can keep creators comfortable. Amit Varma runs a popular course on creative writing. Each cohort gets anywhere from twenty to fifty participants who pay Rs 10,000 or $150; each one runs online over four weekends. Amit has run more than thirty cohorts already.

The principles of the creator economy form the basis of the Career 3.0 archetype.

THIS IS THE BEST TIME TO BECOME A CREATOR

A MOBILE PHONE

FREE SOFTWARE

SOCIAL NETWORKS

REELS

BLOG

VIDEO

PODCAST

CONNECT DIRECTLY TO THE AUDIENCE

NEED ONLY A FEW FANS WILLING TO PAY

A.I. MAKES IT EASY FOR ANYONE TO CREATE GREAT CONTENT

@ABHIJITBHADURI
#CAREER3

Being creative can be financially rewarding

The Creator Economy has become a prominent driver of the Career 3.0 archetype. The independent businesses and side hustles launched by self-employed individuals enable them to make money off their knowledge, skills or following. From vloggers to influencers to writers, creators can monetize themselves, their skills or their creations. The economy also encompasses the companies serving these creators, from content creation tools to analytics platforms.

There are three major reasons why 29 per cent of Gen Z finds the idea of being a creator an attractive option for a career:

a. It offers them the flexibility of not being tied to any one location.
b. It gives them autonomy over their day-to-day choices.
c. Being creative can now be financially rewarding.

In 2018, YouTube was giving 55 per cent of ad revenue to creators. It paid $30 billion to creators for the next three years. Substack writers take home 90 per cent of subscription revenue. Twitch partners collect half of their subscription fees. Patreon creators get paid between 88 per cent to 95 per cent of their subscriptions. OnlyFans creators take home 80 per cent of their earnings.

Companies like Jellysmack and Spotter are offering millions to buy out the old YouTube videos of popular creators. Machine learning algorithms with thousands, or even millions, of data points collected across a bunch of different YouTube channels, that can help them predict just how valuable these will be. And then typically what they'll do is offer cash upfront to that creator, equal to about 80 per cent of what they expect the value of those videos to be, over the next five years. That means the creator can earn millions in royalties.

From toothbrushes to blockbusters: the Career 3.0 journey of Ronnie Screwvala

Ronnie Screwvala has been named among India's most influential and powerful people by publications such as Time, Esquire, *and* Fortune.

Screwvala's career began as a toothbrush manufacturer. In 1981, he made his first foray into the entertainment world by setting up a cable TV business. With an investment of just Rs 37,000, he founded UTV in 1990. UTV went on to produce popular TV shows and commercially successful films.

In 2012, Screwvala sold his share of UTV to Disney for over a billion dollars. Ronnie Screwvala is one of the founders of UpGrad, an online education company. He runs a private equity fund and a sports business. Together, these businesses with his moviemaking work make him the richest filmmaker in India, with a reported net worth of Rs 12,800 crore*.

* DNA Web Team, 'Meet Ronnie Screwvala, Film Producer Who Started Toothbrush Making Unit and Has Net Worth of over Rs 12,800', DNA India, 8 May 2023. https://www.dnaindia.com/bollywood/report-meet-ronnie-screwvala-film-producer-who-started-toothbrush-making-unit-has-net-worth-of-rs-12800-crore-3040949, accessed 4 August 2023.

Screwvala's success can be attributed to his diverse skill set and his ability to learn and adapt to new situations. He has shown an incredible ability to take risks and bounce back from failure. His resilience is an inspiration to all those who aspire to achieve great things in their careers.

Insta reels and influencers in rural India

The creative economy is also making its presence felt in tier-two cities and rural India. Building Instagram reels about farming and matters that impact farmers is creating its own version of influencer marketing. Visual storytelling is a skill that will soon become a price differentiator when someone tries to sell their product or service online. Editing and mixing audio and video clips is generating employment for rural youth.

I spoke to Sumit Saurav who shares the ways the creator economy is drawing in talent from smaller towns in India.

'Firms like PepperContent provide creative services to more than 2,500 firms like Amazon, Swiggy, Indigo, Facebook, Adobe and many more. Most content creators are great at the creative element but need help with business development, finding the right kind of work, negotiating payments etc. That is where PepperContent steps in and becomes a platform for more than 1,00,000 content creators for more than fifty creative service types. These clients ask PepperContent to create videos, posters, website designs etc. and the freelance content creators turn it around. It creates employment for hundreds of creative professionals all over India. Think of it like Urban Company but for creative content. Urban Company provides services for the repair of air conditioners and the services of yoga instructors, plumbers, beauticians and even deep cleaning services,' says Sumit Saurav, who runs ChanceLabs.

ChanceLabs trains the wives of ex-servicemen to join the digital economy because work has become boundaryless. 'Besides building digital skills, we help these ladies to build market awareness, working in teams, storytelling and design thinking. The digital economy is for anyone who has a growth mindset which means you have to believe that you can learn what you do not know yet,' says Saurav.

Translation and subtitling for films, music videos and other kinds of content create opportunities for those with literary flair. Studios are outsourcing colour grading, 3D rendering, visual effects (called VFX for short) as well. Youngsters use software like Blender or Unity to deliver the work. 3D mock-ups of homes and offices are regularly being done in places like Jabalpur and Dindigul for use in mobile games.

On the back of growing marketing and sales across segments, job profiles such as business development executives (500 per cent), field sales executives (374 per cent), digital promoters (200 per cent), brand promoters (75 per cent), and micro influencers (50 per cent) have seen a huge spike in demand for the gig segment. With the post pandemic reset, more and more companies are hiring freelancers for such job roles in the hopes of meeting their yearly targets. Last mile delivery executives have also witnessed a remarkable increase in demand in the recent past, while the demand for tele-callers has also increased considerably.[*]

Case: From homemaker to AI analyst

Pushpa is a thirty-three-year-old homemaker-turned-AI analyst. She grew up in a village in Tamil Nadu where she completed Class XII and got married a few years later. She lives in Bengaluru with her husband who works as a head clerk in the Army Service Corps College Centre. Pushpa was always determined to make a mark of her own but was hesitant to put aside her responsibilities at home and focus on her career. She did not give up the idea of pursuing a career.

When Chance Labs announced their 'Work From Anywhere' training programme for army wives to become AI data analysts, Pushpa was the first one to register and take a chance! Her family was impressed with her initiative. The flexibility to work from anywhere and at any time was a big enabler.

Pushpa and twenty other women joined the Chance Labs programme. She missed a fortnight of training mid-way after the sudden demise of her brother. She returned, even more determined to make up for lost time. It was a promise she had made to her brother long ago. It was time to make good on the promise.

---

[*] India Press Release, 'Gig Jobs See Surge in Demand for Sales and Marketing Roles: Taskmo Gig Index', Press Release, 16 June 2022, https://india-press-release.com/gig-jobs-see-surge-in-demand-for-sales-and-marketing-roles-taskmo-gig-index/, accessed on 4 August 2023.

Pushpa wanted to learn about data labelling. She would diligently practise what she learnt until she was perfect. She was taught digital skills, business communication, presentation skills and AI training. Her speed and attention to detail impressed the recruiters during the employment interviews.

Pushpa made it to the top ten candidates selected from the cohort to join IndiVillage as a contract worker for analysing and training data that is further used to train various algorithms—detecting human diseases early, processing car insurance claims, and more. Today, she owns a laptop and is pursuing her career as an AI analyst. Her ambition is to support her mother with her salary!

Become a creator—even if you are employed somewhere today

The creator economy, also known as the Influencer Economy, refers to the growing trend of individuals using social media platforms and other online channels to create and share content that resonates with their audience. These creators are often considered experts in their field, and their content is seen as valuable and reliable by their followers.

While the Creator Economy is often associated with entrepreneurship and self-employment, there are several ways in which learning from creators can help people even when they are employed.

Learning from creators can help people develop a growth mindset. Creators are often focused on learning and growth, and their content can be a great source of ideas and inspiration for personal and professional development.

By following creators who are focused on learning and growth, you can develop a growth mindset and be more open to new opportunities and challenges.

Living the creator life—this is for every one of us

1. **Creators are constantly learning:** Firstly, learning from creators can help people develop new skills and knowledge. Many creators are constantly learning and sharing new information and insights with their audience. By following creators in your field or related industries, you can learn about new trends, technologies and best practices that can help you stay current and competitive in your career.

2. **Staying at the cutting edge of the profession:** Secondly, learning from creators can help people stay up to date on industry trends. The Creator Economy is constantly evolving. Staying current on trends is essential for success. By following creators who are at the forefront of their field, you can learn about new trends and technologies that could impact your industry and career.

3. **A strong personal brand gets you discovered:** Personal branding is increasingly important in today's job market. There may be thousands of people who have the same job title that you have. What makes you different? Personal branding helps you do just that. You need a strong personal brand to get discovered. Creators often share tips and strategies for building a personal brand. By following and learning from them, you can develop your own personal brand and differentiate yourself in the job market.

4. **Become part of a large professional ecosystem**: Introverts are often at a disadvantage when it comes to networking and connecting with people who can offer opportunities for collaboration. Content creators naturally create communities of followers. By following and interacting with them, you can build your own professional network and connect with others in your industry. This can be especially valuable if you are looking to make a career change or explore new opportunities.

5. **Get inspired and motivated**: Learning from creators can help people stay motivated and inspired. Creators are often driven and passionate about their work, and their content can be a great source of motivation and inspiration. By following creators who are passionate about their work, you can stay motivated and inspired to pursue your own career goals. Learning from creators can help people be more productive. Many creators share tips and strategies for productivity and time management. By following and learning from them, you can develop your own productivity habits and be more effective in your career.

Learning from creators can help people build their online presence. In today's digital age, having an online presence is increasingly important, and creators can be a great source of inspiration and guidance for building an online presence. By following and learning from creators who are successful at building their online presence, you can develop your own online presence and increase your visibility in your industry.

Creators can help people stay engaged and interested in their work. Following creators who are passionate about their work and sharing their insights and experiences can be a great way to stay engaged and interested in your own work. This can be especially important if you are feeling burnt out or unfulfilled in your current career.

From developing new skills and knowledge to building a personal brand, staying up to date on industry trends, and learning from creators can be a valuable resource for anyone looking to advance their career and succeed in today's job market.

TO GATHER COURAGE BEFORE A CAREER SHIFT

TRAVEL

SPEND TIME WITH LOVED ONES

FOCUS ON YOUR HEALTH

SPEND TIME DOING WHAT YOU HAD NO TIME TO PURSUE

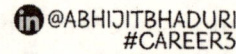 @ABHIJITBHADURI
#CAREER3

Ten things I learnt about attaining financial freedom

1. **Create a budget**: The first step towards financial freedom is to understand your income and expenses. Create a budget that outlines how much money you have coming in and going out each month. This will help you identify areas where you can cut back and save more money.

2. **Pay off debt**: High levels of debt can be a major obstacle to achieving financial freedom. Focus on paying off high-interest debt first, such as credit card debt, and consider consolidating your loans to lower your overall monthly payments.

3. **Build an emergency fund**: Having an emergency fund can help you weather financial setbacks and reduce the need to rely on credit. Aim to save enough to cover at least three to six months' worth of expenses.

4. **Invest in your education**: Investing in your education can help you build skills and knowledge that can lead to higher paying job opportunities. Consider taking courses or earning a degree in a field that aligns with your interests and career goals.

5. **Diversify your income streams**: Having multiple sources of income can help increase your financial stability and provide more flexibility to pursue your dreams. Consider starting a side business or looking for opportunities to earn extra income through freelance work or rental properties.

6. **Automate your savings**: Setting up automatic savings plans can help you save money without having to think

about it. Consider setting up automatic transfers to a savings account or investing in a long-term fund.

7. **Cut expenses**: Look for opportunities to cut unnecessary expenses from your budget. This could include cancelling subscriptions, negotiating lower rates on bills, or finding ways to save on groceries and other every day expenses.

8. **Increase your income**: Look for ways to increase your income, whether through negotiating a raise at your current job or exploring new job opportunities. Consider developing new skills or earning a certification that could make you more competitive in the job market.

9. **Create a financial plan**: Developing a financial plan can help you set clear goals. This will serve as a road map for achieving financial freedom. This can include setting long-term financial goals, such as saving for retirement or paying off debt, as well as short-term goals, like saving for a down payment on a home.

10. **Seek professional advice**: Consider seeking professional financial advice, whether from a financial planner or a financial coach. They can help you develop a financial plan and provide guidance on how to achieve your financial goals.

10

Six Skills for Career 3.0

That everyone needs to build—even if you are employed

Skill No. 1: The ability to build expertise—depth and breadth

Cal Newport, author of the book *So Good They Can't Ignore You,* says that becoming a grandmaster at your work requires years of practice and development of your skills. The greatest experts rarely achieve success solely on the strength of their talent or intelligence. Musicians, doctors and even writers must practise a long time before they can succeed. In the case of doctors, they learn the theory, then observe experienced doctors as they diagnose patients, check the diagnostic tests and discuss the findings with other peers across disciplines. Variations of this process take place in other disciplines.

Expertise is built through repetition and focus. Indian classical musicians practise the nuances of music by singing just a few notes for hours or even days and weeks until their guru gives them a nod of approval.

A musician friend told me that she first learnt Raga Malhar that is said to bring rains and is traditionally played before or during the monsoons. The day she started her lessons, it was raining, and the guru said that he would teach her the Raga Malhar because she would find it easy to remember the association. Over the next two years, she learned many variations of Raga Malhar like Gaud Malhar, Ramadasi Malhar, Miyan ki Malhar, Megh Malhar, Dhulia Malhar and Sawani Malhar. With each variation, she built her expertise so she could learn many other ragas. To the untrained listener, they all sound the same. It takes a lot of skill to differentiate between them.

An expert fashion designer can differentiate between different shades of black e.g., ebony black, charcoal black, midnight black etc. To the layperson, they look the same. Discover the equivalent of the 'seven shades of black' in your profession and become an expert in distinguishing between them.

Here are ten ways to build your expertise:

1. **Break it down.** Break the project down into small, achievable steps and set specific goals that you can work towards, one step at a time. It is easier to master one single line of a song than the entire opera. The key strategy is deliberate practice, which involves setting specific, measurable and challenging goals, and then

focusing on practising the skills needed to achieve those goals with feedback and reflection.

2. **Create an email account for learning**. Look for opportunities to learn from a variety of sources, including books, articles, lectures, courses, and practical experience. Create a new email account and use it to sign up on YouTube, Twitter, Spotify etc. The algorithms will push out content on that topic. You can then consume multiple perspectives of the same topic.

3. **Practise regularly**. The more you practise, the better you will become. Find ways to apply what you are learning in real-world situations, whether through internships, projects, or just working on personal projects.

4. **Collaborate with others**. Work with others who have expertise in different areas, as this can help you learn from their perspectives and experiences. For example, if you are a computer scientist, consider collaborating with a psychologist on a project that combines your respective areas of expertise.

5. **Seek out mentors**. Find people who are experts in your field and ask them for guidance and advice. They can provide valuable insights and help you avoid pitfalls along the way.

6. **Attend conferences and workshops**. Conferences and workshops can be great opportunities to learn from experts in your field, network with others, and stay up to date on the latest research and developments.

7. **Leverage video and audio**. Make a habit of reading papers, articles and blogs in your field to stay up to date on the latest research and developments. Listening to

podcasts and watching videos made by experts can help build powerful learning habits.

8. **Seek feedback**. Ask an expert to give you feedback on what you need to do to get better. Track your progress. Reflect on your mistakes and think about what you can learn from them. Tracking the timing of each lap is a great way to know how much you are improving.

9. **Take on challenges**. Seek out challenges and stretch yourself to learn new things. This can help you grow and develop your expertise.

10. **Teach others**. When you teach, you receive feedback and questions from your students that can challenge your own understanding. This can help you to identify areas where you may have gaps in your knowledge. Plugging those gaps will keep deepening your expertise.

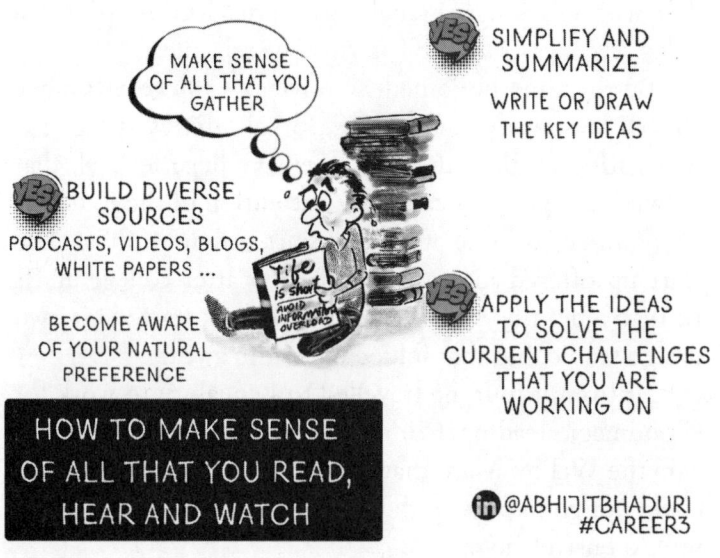

Case: Ritwik Roy

Ritwik Roy is thirty-three now. He was seventeen when he was paid for completing his first freelance project. He was in the eleventh grade and had taught himself Photoshop to create desktop wallpapers for himself and his friends. He and his brother Rahul were football fans and Ritwik enjoyed designing posters and T-shirts for his brother's hostel gang at IIT-Mumbai.

'I redesigned my friend's father's website at his request, over the course of three months. It gave me a chance to learn Hypertext Markup Language (HTML), Cascading Style Sheet (CSS) and JavaScript. In today's terminology, you could say I had done User Interface (UI), User Experience (UX) and full stack front end development. No one in my family has ever pursued a career in graphic design or web design. I taught myself this stuff mostly from video screencasts on the Internet,' he tells me.

By the time he joined St Xavier's College, Mumbai, Ritwik was everyone's choice for all things design. It was during Malhar, the St Xavier's College festival, that Ritwik's design skills caught the attention of the founders of zoomin.com—one of the first start-ups in Mumbai. The start-up offered him a part-time job after college at Rs 10,000 a month. A few years later, Ritwik started his own design studio, but that folded up within a year.

At twenty-four, he travelled to Bengaluru to work for Cloudmagic, leading their iOS design team. Their iOS app won the Webby award that year for best visual design. 'We could not go to pick up the award because the flights were too expensive!' he says.

At twenty-six, Ritwik was back in Mumbai where he met a fellow Apple fanboy and long-time school friend, Parmeet, whose family ran a real-estate firm. Parmeet had recently returned from the US with degrees from Yale and Columbia. He introduced Ritwik to the work of the young Danish iconoclast, architect Bjarke Ingels and told him that they needed to build the architecture team for the firm.

Ritwik took up the offer and decided to study architecture. Vidhi was the first intern in their team. She had a degree in architecture from one of the leading colleges in Mumbai. She became Ritwik's first architecture professor. Ritwik's second professor was Jay, a fresh graduate of the Centre for Environmental Planning and Technology (CEPT), Ahmedabad.

'He joined our firm and got me hooked on to the theory of architecture. Whatever he taught me was then supplemented by reading books and watching videos on YouTube. Our next hire, Sanket, also a CEPT alumnus, taught me the importance of volume in architecture. Even though I'm a partner in the firm, I'm at my best when I am modelling and designing. After seven years of doing theory and hands-on work, it is safe to say that I have a bachelor's degree or maybe a master's degree in architecture,' he adds, with a laugh.

'In 2018, Vidhi and Ritwik started Imagine Café—which became one of the earliest 100 per cent vegan restaurant in Mumbai. Ritwik turned vegan and that forced me to try out new recipes. He would invite me to try out his recipes and give him feedback because he had forgotten the taste of cheese!' says Vidhi. Meanwhile they were using their knowledge of architecture to design that cafe and sharpen their skills of entrepreneurship. Once the cafe was up and running, they decided to hire a team to manage it. Ritwik and Vidhi were married by then.

Then COVID-19 happened. In January 2022, the couple decided to shut down Imagine Café. Would he wish to revive that project in future? I ask him. Ritwik just shrugs.

Just one last bit about Ritwik. During the pandemic, he wanted to sharpen his back-end coding skills. The result was an Enterprise Resource Planning (ERP) system that he built for Sunset, the real estate firm that he co-founded with his friend Parmeet. It's written in Ruby—'a delightful programming language'—and has become a behemoth of a codebase, clocking in at over 15,000 lines of code!

Ritwik speaks of his system with a hint of pride, 'It manages all our expenses, our accounting, site activities and salaries, even the sales and post-sales workflows are routed through the system. I am confident that is the least wobbly ERP system ever built!'

Deliberate practice

Deliberate practice refers to a specific type of practice that involves a high level of focus and effort, with the goal of improving performance in a particular skill or field. This approach to practice is often used by individuals who aspire to become experts in their respective fields. Deliberate practice is used to bring the weaknesses into sharp focus and to keep practising repeatedly until the specific flaws are fixed.

It is better to practise a small aspect of a skill for an extended period of time than to try to master the entire skill at once.

One example of a field where deliberate practice can be applied is music. Professional musicians often spend hours each day practising their instruments, focusing on specific, complex pieces of music. They break down a difficult passage into smaller components and work on each one individually until they can play it flawlessly. By focusing on the most challenging aspects of their music, musicians can gradually improve their technique and overall performance.

Swedish psychologist Anders Ericsson studied the habits of top performers in various fields like music, sports, and chess. Deliberate practice was a common factor among individuals who had achieved the highest levels of performance in their fields.

Basketball players might focus on practising their shooting techniques by taking hundreds of shots each day from different positions on the court. Through deliberate practice, athletes can develop the muscle memory and mental focus needed to perform at the highest level.

Use a coach to break down the various components of the task. Ask for feedback to identify the exact steps you need to fix. Then repeatedly practice that flawed segment till it is perfect.

Bruce Lee's famous quote explains it best: 'I fear not the man who has practiced 10,000 kicks once, but I fear the man who has practiced one kick 10,000 times.'

Skill No. 2: Tell a story—do not give just the information

Storytelling is the art of making the truth fascinating and interesting.

In a world where devices generate data in real time and even churn out analysis, we need humans to make sense of the data. Telling someone that the diamond was 6 cm long means nothing until they are told that the diamond is about the size of an egg. A story finds mind space amid the clutter of data and information like the toddler who finds a space to play even in a crowded train. That is what stories can do.

Stories help us connect the dots between the millions of pieces of information that we get bombarded with every day.

Storytelling is an important part of building the organizational culture because it helps people to relate to a subject and capture the tribal knowledge that employees build over time. Business schools use case studies which are stories of businesses and the choices made by the people in that organization.

A story starts with a description of the current situation; then it introduces a complication or conflict or a problem within the existing situation; the story ends with the resolution of the conflict.

But what is a story?

A story sets the listener's imagination on fire.

Everyone likes a good story. No one likes information and chunks of data thrown at them. People want that information to be conveyed in a manner that will linger on in their minds long after. You heard the story of the hare and the tortoise years ago, but the lesson remains fresh— 'slow and steady wins the race'.

Chances are that you even remember the drawing that accompanied the story. Stories have a way of etching themselves in our minds.

Case: Amit Varma on being a professional storyteller

Amit Varma won the prestigious Bastiat Prize for Journalism in 2007 and 2015, becoming the first person to win it twice. In 2009, Business Week named him one of the 50 Most Powerful People in India.

His blog, India Uncut, was one of India's most popular blogs in the years it was active, between 2004 and 2008. He was a serious poker player for a few years and wrote a column on poker called Range Rover for the *Economic Times*. He also hosts the weekly podcast, The Seen and the Unseen, which gets over 2,25,000 downloads a month.

How did he become a professional storyteller? I asked him.

The early days: I wanted to be a writer.

Amit Varma started off on what may seem like a Career 1.0 journey when he decided very early that he wanted to be a writer. He wanted to become an advertising copywriter or a television scriptwriter and then become a journalist as a path to becoming a full-time writer. Then blogging became a thing.

Then I wanted to be a blogger.

In the 1990s and early 2000s, things started to evolve. At that time, Amit regularly wrote India Uncut, which became really popular. It was a labour of love. At that time, he was struck by a few things.

'I was then the managing editor of Cricinfo, but I wanted to write about other things besides cricket. Blogging was attractive; it helped me break away from traditional writing formats. I was no longer bound to write 800 words or adhere to the standard lengths. I wasn't tied to the news cycle. I could write whatever I wanted. I wasn't tied to any house style; I could write in any way I wanted and find my voice. I wasn't tied by demands or limitations of any kind. I've blogged five posts a day for five years and notched up some 8000 posts. I did those 8000 posts even though there was no money coming in because I just enjoyed doing it.'

Repetition helps you get better at your craft.

If you do what you enjoy, it leads to excellence, because you can do something again and again. When we start doing something new, we are awful at it, because our skills are limited. A lot of creators want approval and validation from day one. They overestimate the short-term and underestimate the long-term.

So, in the short term, they think that they will do a podcast and a YouTube video and become stars overnight.

But that's not how it works out. Initially your skill combination is inadequate. Even if your skills are great, there is no validation because your following is limited. Growing your follower base will take time and you must live without validation. If you persevere, it will make you excellent. Do what you love, because that's the only way you'll keep doing it even if there is no feedback, even if no one's watching.

You build followership and credibility before you make money. Amit Varma summarizes his own journey, 'In my blogging days, I did not make money, but it built my following and my credibility. *Mint* asked me to write a column for them. *Wall Street Journal* then asked me to write for them. I won the Bastiat Prize for Journalism in 2007.

'With podcasting, I started *The Seen and the Unseen* five years ago. It was an experiment. For more than 100 episodes, I made no money. But it was a labour of love for me. I didn't expect anything. I thought I'd experiment. As I got deeper into it and the show evolved, I realized that I loved doing it. This is worth doing for its own sake and so I stuck to it.'

Amit is proof that success in Career 3.0 comes with fame and recognition. You make as much or more as you would in any other profession. Amit's weekly podcast *The Seen and the Unseen* crossed more than 350 episodes at the end of 2022.

He runs four classes on writing every month.

'That alone is enough to live well in Mumbai,' he says.

HOW TO TURN INFORMATION INTO STORIES

1 SIMPLIFY YOUR IDEA - NO MORE THAN 3 IDEAS

2 WHY AND HOW THIS SOLVES A PROBLEM THE AUDIENCE HAS

3 AFTER YOU MAKE THE SLIDES, SHARE IT WITH PEOPLE UNFAMILIAR WITH YOUR IDEA. ASK THEM TO RECALL THE SLIDES.

4 REDO THE SLIDES

PRACTISE TELLING THE STORY. THAT IS WHAT THE AUDIENCE REMEMBERS

@ABHIJITBHADURI
#CAREER3

Let us get a quick primer on using storytelling to understand your career plan!

Using 'The Pixar Structure' to talk about your Career 3.0 strategy

You may be surprised to learn that a skill used in business messaging can also help you when discerning whether an additional job, or an entire change of career, may be right for you. When considering a career move, it helps to get clarity so that you know where you are headed and if it's something that will make you happy. It's a great way to project yourself into the future to see what a change of career may look like.

Douglass and Lisa-Marie Hatcher, co-founders of the business storytelling training firm, communicate4IMPACT, share the following insights and examples:

When considering whether a career change (or variation) might be right for you, a classic storytelling structure called the Once Upon a Time structure (aka 'The Pixar Structure') can be very useful.

The Pixar Structure can help you in three ways:

1. It can help you get clarity on what makes you happiest and what a change of career might look like.
2. It can help you explain the thinking behind a career shift to family and friends.
3. It's also a great way to create an elevator pitch for potential clients or customers if you do make the change.

The 'Once Upon a Time/Pixar structure' goes like this:

Step 1. ONCE UPON A TIME. This is the current situation.

Step 2. AND EVERY DAY. This is the recurring problem.

Step 3. UNTIL ONE DAY. This is your intervening solution.

Step 4. BECAUSE OF THAT. Benefit or Payoff #1.

Step 5. BECAUSE OF THAT. Benefit or Payoff #2.

Step 6. BECAUSE OF THAT. Benefit or Payoff #3.

Step 7. UNTIL FINALLY. Resolution to the problem.

Exercise: Using the Pixar framework to re-evaluate what makes you happy

How a VP in a biosciences company is re-evaluating what makes her happy using the Pixar framework of storytelling:

1.   Once Upon a Time . . .

I work in corporate communications for a multinational biosciences company. I've been in my current role as VP of reputation management for three years.

I've survived two reorganizations and been promoted twice. I remind myself that things could be worse. But when I'm being honest with myself, I realize there aren't any substantial advancement opportunities on the horizon. And if I'm being really honest, I feel sort of stuck.

I even asked my immediate manager about professional development opportunities, only to learn that there are waiting lists to get into the courses that I'm interested in.

2.   And Every Day

This hamster wheel existence has been taking its toll on me for a while. Each morning, when I wake up, I don't dread going to work, but I don't have the kind of excitement I'd like to have either. In a perfect world, I'd like to do more than simply go through the motions to get a comfortable pay cheque.

3.   Until One Day

One evening, I decided to jot down a few thoughts in my journal. I used to do this every night, but lately, I haven't been motivated enough. I grabbed a pen, opened my journal, and began to write an entry for the day that had passed. I began to capture some of what I had been thinking and experiencing for the last few months. Ten, or maybe fifteen minutes, went by, and all of a sudden, for the first time in a while, I felt like myself again.

4. Because of That

I began to flip back to previous journal entries.

5. Because of That

I saw an entry from a year ago titled: My Perfect Day Doing My Perfect Job. The perfect job, for me, was being a guitar instructor with my own YouTube channel.

6. Because of That

I then started thinking about what a perfect day could look like as a guitar teacher on YouTube. That perfect day would involve a teaching schedule that kept me busy and created income as well.

7. Until Finally

I began to assess my work trajectory and thought about the skills I had developed over the years. And I wondered if the skills in my current role could help me create my own business as a guitar teacher.

How to use storytelling structures to create a start-up pitch

Whether your start-up has thousands of employees or just you, it needs a pitch deck. The pitch deck is powerful because it can be used to speak to employees that you wish to hire. The same story structure can be used to create an elaborate pitch deck when you are trying to raise funds from VCs. The story structure remains the same.

Once Upon a Time

I had been in my corporate communications job for three years and felt stuck.

And Every Day

Each morning, when I woke up, I didn't dread going to work, but I didn't have the kind of excitement I wanted to have either.

Until One Day

Then one day, I was flipping through my journal and saw an old entry titled, My Perfect Day Doing My Perfect Job, which was being a YouTube guitar instructor.

Because of That

It reminded me of how much joy my guitar had given me over the years.

Because of That

I decided to give myself permission to explore a change of career.

Because of That

I sketched out a plan of what my dream job might look like. I wasn't prepared to quit my full-time, day job—but I was prepared to try something new on the side.

Until Finally

And so, I created a YouTube channel, providing free instructional guitar videos to people like you.

Douglass and Lisa-Marie's powerful application of a well-known story structure is a wonderful way to map out your Career 3.0.

Master storyteller Jean-Luc Godard had said, 'A story should have a beginning, a middle, and an end, but not necessarily in that order.'

Example: How to use storytelling structures to pitch your book to a publisher

I used the same storyline structure when I pitched my book on hiring to potential publishers. You can use the same structure to pitch your book to a publisher.

The title of my book was *Don't Hire the Best*.

Once Upon a Time

We all make people decisions every day. From choosing a tutor for the kids to hiring a CEO, people take bets on people.

And Every Day

The most common way to hire someone is to interview them.

Until One Day

But most people are terrible at interviewing.

Because of That

An interview is actually a test of the interviewer—not the interviewee.

Because of That

No two people do the same job with the same results. Two successive CEOs in the same company can have different results. We need to evaluate the personality of the candidate. Skills can be learnt.

Because of That

The evaluation of personality is a more stable, scientific method upon which to base hiring decisions.

Until Finally

I can share a simple framework that will help you understand how to hire better. You don't need to hire the 'best' person for the job; you have to hire the 'right' person for the job.

This storytelling structure can be a very powerful way for you to formulate your plans or even create your elevator pitch. Try it out and I guarantee you that the results will be delightful.

Skill No. 3: The ability to teach online

Imagine that you had to teach people how to use Microsoft Excel. What is the most creative way to teach others how to use this software?

In June 2020, Kat Norton posted her first video online. This was a time when she was staring at a huge amount of student debt. At age twenty-seven, working as a consultant did not seem to give her the kind of financial freedom that she wanted. Her videos changed everything when she started teaching little tips and tricks on Microsoft Excel through her catchy videos on TikTok.

You make it fun; we make you rich: Known as @kat_norton on TikTok, she is now an influencer with more than 10,00,000 followers on social media. She combines everything from electronic dance music to cooking recipes as a way to explain Microsoft Excel features and people cannot have enough of her. Her TikTok videos are often creative and visually appealing, using a mix of animation, graphics, and real-life examples to illustrate complex concepts in a way that is easy to understand. In addition to her talent for teaching, Norton also has a warm and friendly personality that makes her relatable and approachable to her audience.

Ability to simplify: One of the things that sets Norton apart from other Excel influencers is her ability to break down complex topics into bite-sized, easy-to-follow lessons. She is skilled at explaining things in a clear and concise manner, and she uses real-world examples to help viewers see how they can apply what they are learning to their own lives.

In addition to her Excel tutorials, Norton also creates content that covers a wide range of topics related to productivity, organization and personal development. She shares tips and strategies for staying organized and motivated, as well as advice for managing time and increasing efficiency.

In January 2021, she quit her job in corporate America to run her nine courses online. In ten months, she was making $1,00,000 a day. Did I tell you that she works four hours a day and makes approximately $2 million a year?*

She's been doing this since June 2020. It took her six months to make $1,00,000. Soon she was making $1,00,000 a month. The next logical step was to start making $1,00,000 a day. To put this in perspective,

---

* Norton, Kat, 'I Work Just 4 Hours a Day: This 29-Year-Old's Side Hustle Brings in $2 Million a Year—a Look at Her Typical Day', CNBC, 26 December 2022, https://www.cnbc.com/2022/12/26/this-29-year-olds-side-hustle-brings-in-2-million-a-year-i-work-4-hours-a-week.html, accessed on 4 August 2023.

an average teacher in public schools in the US makes approximately $55,000 a year.

There are three big lessons to be learned from her success story:

1. Become a community builder; engage and communicate with the community regularly.
2. Being authentic helps to build trust among viewers in a manner that is more sustainable.
3. Choose something where you can have fun even if you have to do it every single day.

She says, 'I host these different high-energy Excel parties, essentially, where I come in and I teach a ton of free content. If you look at my page, I'm just giving away knowledge because my social media presence is what draws people in. That's my purpose: to provide as much value to people as possible. That's why I host these Excel training sessions and offer a deal on my products at the end of the webinar.'

Case: Faisal Khan aka Khan Sir

Fazal Khan is better known as 'Khan Sir' in Patna, where he has gained a reputation for his innovative and engaging teaching style, has helped him to become one of the most popular teachers in the country.

One of the things that sets thirty-one-year-old Khan Sir apart from other teachers is his ability to make complex concepts easy to understand. He has a talent for breaking down difficult topics into simple, digestible chunks of information, which make his classes accessible and enjoyable for students at all levels.

In addition to his teaching skills, Khan Sir is also known for his dedication to his students. He is always willing to go the extra mile to help them succeed, whether it's staying after class to provide extra help or offering one-on-one tutoring sessions. This dedication has earned him a loyal following of students who are grateful for his guidance and support.

Flexibility: Online courses can be taught from anywhere with an Internet connection, allowing for a great deal of flexibility in terms of location and schedule. Teaching online requires much more preparation and coordination.

Wider reach: Online courses can be accessed by students from anywhere in the world, allowing you to reach a much larger audience than you would be able to in a traditional classroom setting.

Greater control over the learning environment: As the instructor, you have greater control over the learning environment in an online course. This includes being able to customize the course content, materials and delivery methods to best suit your students' needs.

Increased accessibility: Online courses can be more accessible for students with disabilities or other challenges that might make it difficult for them to attend a traditional classroom.

Self-paced learning: Online courses allow students to work at their own pace, which can be beneficial for those who prefer to work faster or slower than the average pace of a traditional classroom would allow.

Cost-effectiveness: Online courses can be more cost-effective for both students and instructors, as they often require fewer resources and may be delivered more efficiently.

Opportunities for collaboration: Online courses often incorporate tools and platforms that facilitate collaboration and interaction among students and instructors, allowing for a more engaging and interactive learning experience.

Increased engagement: Online courses can be more engaging for students due to the interactive nature of many of the tools and platforms used in their delivery.

Convenience: Online courses offer a high level of convenience for both students and instructors, as they can be accessed and completed from any device with an Internet connection.

Professional development: Teaching an online course can be a great way to develop new skills and knowledge, as well as to demonstrate expertise in a particular subject. It can also be a valuable addition to your CV, particularly if you are seeking to advance in your career.

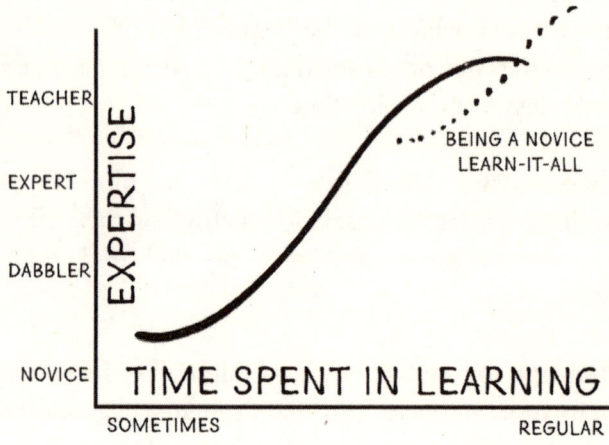

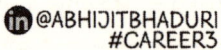

@ABHIJITBHADURI
#CAREER3

Skill No. 4: The ability to be part of multiple ecosystems

We grow up as part of different ecosystems. Our extended family, the neighbourhood, the friends we make in college or at work, all represent different ecosystems.

Networking is the process of making and maintaining connections with other individuals or organizations for the purpose of sharing information, resources and opportunities. It involves building relationships with people who may be able to provide support, guidance, or referrals in your personal or professional life.

Networking can take many different forms, including attending events or conferences, joining professional organizations or social groups, connecting with others through social media platforms, or reaching out to individuals through email or other forms of communication. The aim of networking is to build a network of contacts that can help you achieve your goals and advance your career or personal interests.

Building relationships across diverse ecosystems involves connecting and collaborating with individuals and organizations across different fields, industries, or areas of expertise to create new and innovative solutions to complex problems. This is different from networking, which focuses primarily on building connections and relationships within a specific industry or field.

In diverse ecosystems, individuals and organizations bring different perspectives, experiences and knowledge to the table. Building relationships across these diverse ecosystems requires individuals to be open-minded, adaptable and willing to learn from others who have different perspectives and experiences. We need to actively seek out opportunities to connect with others, participate in collaborative projects or initiatives, and work together to find solutions to complex problems.

A professional actor or sportsperson can teach you how to bounce back from failure because they experience success and failure in rapid succession. A hit and a flop can both happen in the same year. The cricketer who was idolized upon winning a match can be abused and booed when he disappoints his fans. An actor can work with an accountant friend to become better at negotiating contracts.

When it comes to being part of multiple ecosystems, I had to think of KPR.

Case: KPR—from employment to entrepreneurship to politics and back

K. Pandiarajan (popularly known as KPR) is a business leader in India. He was a classmate of mine at XLRI, Jamshedpur. After a bachelor's degree in engineering, he did a postgraduate degree in personnel management and industrial relations. He then pursued a career in corporate India for a few years.

A decade after being in the corporate world, the entrepreneurial bug bit him. Ma Foi Management Consultants was set up by KPR and his wife Latha. They built it into one of the largest HR service providers in the country. Ma Foi created employment opportunities for more than 4,00,000 professionals in thirty-six countries with offices all over India besides fourteen other countries. KPR set up an educational trust and the Ma Foi Foundation that has touched the lives of more than 1,00,000 families through its education, healthcare and livelihood schemes. KPR became actively involved in Corporate Social Responsibility (CSR) activities that focus on empowering children, women, and youth through education, healthcare and livelihood support.

Then one day I heard that KPR had joined Tamil Nadu politics. He became a member of the Legislative Assembly (MLA) in 2011.

In 2016, he was re-elected and became a minister in the state of Tamil Nadu, handling the portfolios of school education, youth and sports, culture and Tamil development.

After a decade in politics, KPR is back to being an entrepreneur. He is the chairman of the new-age HR services company, CIEL HR, which offers recruitment, staffing and HR consultancy services across India. He has also written two books in Tamil.

What did he enjoy more—the stint in politics, being an entrepreneur or being an employee in corporate India?

'It is the scale of the impact that is exciting rather than the stint,' says KPR.

'Does that mean that you intend to return to politics?' I ask him.

'Why can't all of it be done together? I can be in politics, be an entrepreneur, an author and run the CSR trust. Life is too short to do just one thing,' he says.

Ecosystems are built by many members of interdisciplinary teams

The community consists of different kinds of professionals who support each other. As work becomes more complex, we need to dig into ecosystems in order to build multi-disciplinary understanding.

Becoming part of a community or an ecosystem can be an important part of your professional development and growth. A community or ecosystem is a group of individuals or organizations that are connected and support each other in a particular field or industry. Community members gain access to valuable resources, expertise, and opportunities that can help them succeed.

1. **Access to resources and expertise:** Communities and ecosystems often provide access to resources and

expertise that can help you grow and develop in your career. This can include access to training, mentorship, and networking opportunities, as well as resources like research materials, industry publications, and software tools.

2. **Collaboration and support**: Being part of a community or ecosystem can provide a sense of support and collaboration, which can be especially important if you're working in a field that requires a lot of independent work. Communities can provide a sense of camaraderie and a sense of belonging, which can help you stay motivated and focused on your goals.

3. **Opportunities for growth and advancement**: Communities and ecosystems often provide opportunities for growth and advancement, such as networking events, job openings, or speaking engagements. By building relationships with other members of the community, you can increase your visibility and access to new opportunities.

So, how can you become part of a community or ecosystem? Here are a few steps you can take:

Identify your goals: Before you start looking for a community to join, it's important to identify your goals and what you hope to gain from being part of a community. This will help you find a community that is aligned with your values and career objectives.

Research communities in your field: Look for communities or ecosystems in your field or industry. You can do this by searching online, attending industry events, or reaching out to professionals in your field for recommendations.

Engage with the community: Once you've found a community that is aligned with your goals, start engaging with it. This can include attending events, participating in online discussions, or volunteering your time or expertise.

Build relationships: To become part of a community, one needs to build relationships with other members of the community. Make an effort to get to know other members and consider reaching out to professionals you admire or respect for mentorship or advice.

Contribute to the community: To become a valued member of a community, it's important to contribute to the community in some way. This can include volunteering your time, sharing your expertise or resources, or providing support to other members of the community.

By following these steps, you can become an active and valuable member of a community or ecosystem that can support your professional development and growth.

Skill No. 5: Building your personal brand

To her countless fans on Instagram, Eshna Kutty is an inspiration. She describes herself on her Instagram bio as a Flow artiste, Hooper, Instructor and an entrepreneur.

Her firm, called hoop.flo, monetizes her hoop classes (that have a waiting list). She endorses brands and travels to various places teaching people how to dance and move while moving the hula hoop around her body.

One of her dance videos went viral and multiple career options opened up for her. She was everywhere—on TV, on her YouTube channel and of course on her Instagram page. Did I tell you that she is also a Psychology graduate?

When the dating app Tinder started its 'mixers' as an opportunity to get singles together after two years of isolation forced by the pandemic, they invited Flo dancer Eshna Kutty to be the brand evangelist.

'I'm a hoop dancer, teacher, facilitator, performer and learner. It's been a ten-year journey, from hula hooping alone in my bedroom to now sharing this flow art with thousands,' says Eshna Kutty. That is what a successful Career 3.0 looks like.

The what, why and how of personal brands

So, how can you build a strong personal brand? Here are a few tips:

Do you really need to build a personal brand? Until the 1980s, people joined one organization and retired from it with a gift and a pension. A couple of forces have converged to change that. The result is the fading away of the notion of a steady job. Over the years, the employment contract between the employer and the employee has been redefined. From a lifetime contract, jobs are now more like short-term contracts. What changed the trend?

McKinsey believes that by 2027, 75 per cent of the companies quoted on the S&P 500, say in 2016, will have disappeared. The average lifespan of companies listed in S&P 500 was sixty-one years in 1958. Today, it is less than eighteen years. That means individuals will need to find ways to be employed by different employers during the course of their career. A strong personal brand makes a candidate even more attractive to a potential employer. The candidate is often headhunted directly.

Your personal brand is the set of adjectives that people use to describe you when you are not in the room. A personal brand exists whether we consciously craft it or not. Here is a simple exercise you can use to uncover your personal brand.

1. Identify a few adjectives that someone needs to have in the job that you aspire to do e.g., adaptable, bold, confident, creative, dependable, playful, analytical, strategic etc.
2. Ask some of your colleagues to choose three qualities that describe you.
3. Now see which of the qualities appear frequently in the list your colleagues described. Do the qualities needed for the job (adaptable, bold, confident, creative, dependable, playful, analytical, strategic) come up frequently when your friends think of you?
4. Your personal brand reflects the adjectives that have come up frequently.
5. Choose the adjectives that did not come up frequently but are essential to the dream job. How can you demonstrate those adjectives in your day-to-day behaviour? Think about that.

Think about yourself: The first step in building a strong personal brand is to think about what makes you unique and valuable. Consider your skills, experiences, values and personal brand statement. A personal brand statement is a short, concise statement that summarizes your brand identity and value proposition.

Establish an online presence: In today's digital age, it's important to establish an online presence to showcase your personal brand. This can include creating a LinkedIn profile, building a personal website, or maintaining a blog or social media accounts.

Network and build relationships: Building relationships with industry leaders and other professionals can help you establish your personal brand and get noticed in your field. Attend industry events, join professional organizations, and make connections on social media to expand your network.

Provide value: To build a strong personal brand, it's important to consistently provide value to your audience or clients. This can include sharing relevant information or insights, offering valuable resources, or providing high-quality products or services.

Be consistent: Consistency is key when it comes to building a strong personal brand. Make sure all of your online profiles, websites and social media accounts have a consistent look and feel, and that your messaging is consistent across all channels.

Getting discovered is just as important for a freelancer as it is for an employee

A personal brand is the unique set of attributes, skills, and experiences that make you stand out in your career or industry. It's the reputation you build for yourself based on your professional achievements, skills and values. A strong personal brand can help you stand out in the job market, attract opportunities, and build credibility and influence in your field.

There are several reasons why having a strong personal brand is important as a career strategy:

1. *It helps you differentiate yourself:* A strong personal brand can help you stand out in a crowded job market or industry, especially if your qualifications are similar to those of other candidates. By establishing a clear brand identity, you can differentiate yourself from the competition and showcase your unique value proposition.
2. *It enhances your reputation:* A strong personal brand can help you build a positive reputation and be seen as a thought leader or expert in your field. This can lead to more opportunities for speaking engagements, consulting work, or partnerships.
3. *It attracts opportunities:* A strong personal brand can attract opportunities for career advancement or new job openings. Employers are often attracted to candidates with a strong personal brand because they see them as a valuable asset to the company.
4. *It helps you build relationships:* A strong personal brand can help you build relationships with potential clients, customers, or partners. By establishing yourself as

a trusted and reliable expert, you can build strong, long-lasting relationships that can help your career or business to grow.

Ten actions you can take to build your brand

1. *Define your brand:* Before you start building your personal brand, it's important to have a clear understanding of what makes you unique and what you want to be known for. Take some time to define your brand and what it stands for.
2. Build a website: Having a website is a great way to showcase your personal brand and provide information about your skills, experience and accomplishments. Consider creating a professional website that includes a portfolio of your work, a blog and contact information.
3. *Use social media:* Social media platforms like LinkedIn, Twitter/X, and Instagram can be powerful tools for building your personal brand. Use these platforms to share your expertise, connect with others, and showcase your work.
4. *Network in person:* In-person networking events can be a great way to build your personal brand and connect with others in your industry. Consider attending conferences, workshops, and other events that align with your interests and goals.
5. *Create valuable content:* Sharing valuable, high-quality content is a great way to build your personal brand and establish yourself as an expert in your field. This can include writing articles, creating videos or sharing your thoughts and insights on social media.

6. *Collaborate with others:* Collaborating with others is a great way to expand your reach and build your personal brand. Look for opportunities to work with other professionals or organizations on projects or initiatives that align with your goals.

7. *Volunteer your time and expertise:* Volunteering your time and expertise is a great way to build your personal brand and make a positive impact in your community. Look for opportunities to volunteer with organizations that align with your interests and goals.

8. *Be authentic:* To build a strong personal brand, it's important to be authentic and genuine. Be yourself and don't try to be someone you're not.

9. *Consistency is key:* Consistency is key when building your personal brand. Use the same logo, colour scheme, and messaging across all your online and offline channels to create a cohesive brand identity.

10. *Seek feedback:* Finally, don't be afraid to seek feedback on your personal brand. Ask others for their thoughts and insights on what you're doing well and where you can improve. This can help you fine-tune your brand and ensure that you're effectively communicating your value and expertise to others.

Skill No. 6: Think like a venture capitalist—plot your skills and projects portfolio

The S-curve is a concept that describes the life cycle of a product or service. It starts with slow growth and then increases at an accelerating rate until it reaches a plateau.

Here's a simple example to help illustrate the S-curve: imagine you are starting a new business to sell a product. You are learning about the product and the customer. This is the phase where you wobble and crave for stability.

As you gain more customers and word spreads about your product, sales will start to increase at a faster rate. Eventually, sales will reach a point where they level off, or plateau, as the market becomes saturated, or a new product or technology takes over.

The rise of smartphones and mobile apps, which have largely replaced traditional desktop computers and software programs, is an example. Someone who was an expert in desktop software development may have been highly sought after a decade ago, but if they have not kept up with the latest developments in mobile technology, they may now be considered irrelevant.

The middle of the S-curve is when your product is growing exponentially. Customers want everything that you make. This is when the firm is at its busiest and there is no time to do anything new. This is when the seeds of decline are sowed in the firm.

The Ambassador car was a popular model of car produced by Hindustan Motors in India from 1958 to 2014. It was based on the Morris Oxford series III, which was produced in the UK from 1956 to 1959. The Ambassador was known for its durability and long-lasting design, which did not change significantly from 1950 to 1990.

However, despite its popularity and enduring design, the Ambassador eventually lost market share to newer, modern models of cars. The lack of significant changes to the Ambassador's design over the years may have contributed to its decline, as consumers increasingly sought out more advanced and feature-rich vehicles.

VCs are experts at identifying and supporting promising start-ups and projects and, by learning to think like one, you can develop the skills and insights needed to make smart investments and achieve success.

One key aspect of thinking like a VC is building and managing a portfolio of investments. Rather than putting all your eggs in one basket, a well-managed portfolio allows you to spread your risk across a diverse range of investments, reducing the impact of any single failure and increasing your chances of overall success.

To build a successful portfolio, it's important to carefully evaluate each potential investment and consider its risk and reward potential. Some investments may be riskier but offer the potential for a higher return, while others may be more stable but offer a lower return. It's up to you to decide how to balance these trade-offs and allocate your resources in a way that maximizes your chances of success.

Managing your risk-reward ratio is another important aspect of thinking like a VC. This means considering the potential risks and rewards of each investment and determining the appropriate level of risk for your portfolio. This might involve taking on more risk in some areas in order to pursue higher returns, while also including more stable investments to balance out this risk.

Overall, thinking like a VC involves developing the skills and insights needed to identify and support promising start-ups and projects, building and managing a diverse portfolio of investments, and carefully considering the risk-reward ratio of each investment. By learning to think like a VC, you can increase your chances of success and achieve your goals.

Case: Jayanti 'Jonty' Rajagopalan

In 1995, a professor asked Jonty's class to write a little something about their dream jobs. Jonty wrote about her dream of curating experiences for travel companies where she would travel the world and get paid for it. She had to wait for thirteen years before she could realize that dream. What else did she do?

1. **Relearn a language she knew**: Learning a new language is often a great metaphor for rewiring the brain to look at situations differently. After her post-graduation in human resources, Jonty got her first job as a personnel executive in the watch factory of Titan Industries Limited. That meant handling the day-to-day leave, loans, medical insurance etc. and other related issues of almost 300 (mostly women) employees in the Assembly Department. 'I thought I knew a lot, including Tamil which was my mother tongue,' she said. She had to learn the way Tamil was spoken in the factory so that she could persuade others and get things done.

2. **Learn to make a career pivot**: Two years later, a restless Jonty made a career pivot. She shifted from HR to sales and marketing. It was like learning a new language. 'I think the ability to learn languages makes it easy for people to remain flexible,' Jonty recalls.

3. **From sales to social impact**: In 2006, Jonty found herself working for the Bill and Melinda Gates

Foundation. Overnight, she found herself standing on blazing hot highways in Andhra Pradesh talking to sex workers and hijras, explaining condom usage. From discussing retail trends and brands and presenting to boardrooms, she found herself listening to the myths surrounding Acquired Immunodeficiency Syndrome (AIDS) among the truckers.

A portfolio of experiences

'My time at the Gates Foundation seemed like a crash course in entrepreneurship,' says Jonty. 'As an entrepreneur, you have to be self-directed and work without supervision.

'This is one of the biggest shifts from being an employee to becoming an entrepreneur. While there is immense freedom, it comes with a disproportionate degree of responsibility.'

In late 2008, Jonty launched Detours India, a Hyderabad-based venture that offers specialized and customized tours for the adventurous traveller.

Talking about her role there, she says, 'On any given day I perform so many roles, from being the president to the peon. I am the courier, and I am also the accountant. I had to get my hands dirty and accept that no job is beneath me within my own organization. I was the face of the company and was also the expert tour guide trying to rebrand the way Hyderabad was presented to the world.'

Don't forget what you know

Summarizing the portfolio of her experiences, Jonty says, 'What I learned in my post-graduation helped me work seamlessly with the factory workers. Learning the dialect so that I could be more effective in communicating with the employees prepared me for the shift from HR to sales and marketing. Travelling with the sales team to different parts of the country, built empathy for the people I dealt with at the Gates Foundation. The cumulative learning gave me the courage to become an entrepreneur and find new ways to grow my business without compromising my values. I reinvented group tours by using some of my HR training or interesting team activities I use in the corporate world.

'While I was running my tours business, I used my knowledge of history and the rich culture of India to design truly unique experiences. Detours started in 2008. Less than thirteen years later, the world changed. COVID-19 struck the whole travel and hospitality industry really hard, and I was forced, this time by external forces, to reinvent myself. I can honestly tell you that none of my learnings could prepare me for the two-and-a-half years of the COVID-19 crisis. This time the reinvention was not a choice.'

Jonty used the time to learn Spanish. She got certified to become a coach. In true Career 3.0 style, she continues to monetize her different skills and skill combinations.

'The last two plus years have given me ample time to look back at my path. In fact, I can even honestly say that this is the first time that I have actually sat back to reflect on my own career in an objective manner. The pandemic and the impact that it has had on my travel business is what led me to yet another crossroads, but this time the challenge and the roadblock was external . . . the need for change did not come from within,' she says.

She has embarked on an exciting journey of bringing together three of her passions—food, travel and sport in order to shape her life to be 'abundant and generous'.

'It is not easy for a middle-class Indian to quit a well-paying job and take up entrepreneurship. There is a lot of risk. There is a lot of uncertainty. And it needs a huge amount of optimism and resilience to survive the highs and lows. The last day as an employee is a haze. The decision to become an entrepreneur is a moment of madness. But without that moment of madness, no adventure can ever begin.' That is Jonty's word of advice.

'Learn to think like a VC,' says Jonty.

VCs invest in multiple start-up ideas. These ideas can range from a diverse set of businesses from the fields of sports, travel, food, edtech etc. to create new offerings. Career 3.0 looks like a pizza with different slices. Each slice represents a different skill that can be monetized. A VC had once told me that only one in ten ventures ever succeed. One single successful idea can subsidize nine other ventures. The VC knows that many of these remaining ventures will fail for a variety of reasons. But they carry on. Regardless.

Think like a VC. Act like them. Carry on.

II

Looking at the Future of Careers

A two-by-two matrix is an incredibly powerful way to sort out anything which has two variables. When it comes to careers, the two variables could be the size of your ambition and the size of the canvas you wish to paint on.

That translates to being a small fish or a big fish to reflect the size of one's ambition. The size of the pond could translate to the kind of employer one is comfortable working for. The same two-by-two matrix could also be useful for an entrepreneur. Someone who is operating out of a garage to create the blueprint of a start-up may be a small fish in a small pond today but could well be the next big fish in the big pond tomorrow.

IDENTIFY YOUR AMBITION SIZE

in @ABHIJITBHADURI
#CAREER3

An archetype is a universal, recurring pattern or theme in literature, art, or psychology that represents a fundamental human experience or instinct. The concept of archetypes was developed by psychologist Carl Jung, who believed that these patterns or themes are present in the collective unconscious of all humans, and that they manifest in our thoughts, feelings, and behaviours.

I hope these three archetypes will make sense to you. The archetypes certainly helped me answer the question that I was asked as a kid, 'What do you want to be when you grow up?'

In 2016, I left the corporate world to live my life as a Career 3.0 professional. My revenue streams came from the different ecosystems I had been a part of.

I worked as a consultant and keynote speaker on leadership, talent, and culture. In this, I drew upon my learning as an HR professional. My consulting projects came together in my writings on LinkedIn, magazines, and newspaper columns. The book *Dreamers and Unicorns* put a framework that made it easy to share my experiences as a consultant and coach. The book created a new revenue stream and in turn provided the springboard for my podcast by the same name. You can listen to the podcasts on Google, Apple, Spotify or any other platforms. The podcast has some fascinating stories about career journeys. I spoke to friends, colleagues, clients and even strangers to ask them about their career journey.

When I noticed the three archetypes, it was hard to stop seeing these everywhere. That is what insight is all about. It is universal and blindingly obvious once you discover it.

I wish you too can use the archetypes to make sense of your journey through life.

Acknowledgements

I am deeply grateful to the team at Penguin Random House who helped transform a rough idea into a polished book.

Karthik, you spotted the potential of the idea of *Career 3.0* in my last book *Dreamers and Unicorns*. This is the second book that we have crafted together. Here's to many more.

Aakriti, your cover design surpassed even AI-created options, and it was a joy to share this on my LinkedIn newsletter. Yash Daiv, your editing skills not only made the copy crisp and engaging, but also brought a clarity and precision that truly elevated the text. Ahana, your creativity and strategic thinking will help this book get noticed. Every author knows that writing a book is never as complicated as placing it in the hands of the reader.

Milee Ashwarya and Gaurav Srinagesh, thank you for creating a publishing powerhouse like Penguin Random House India.

To everyone who shared their career dilemmas and triumphs, thank you. I hope I was able to tell your story accurately. To my colleagues, employers, clients, and friends who have journeyed with me through the world of work, thank you.

To my family who has been with me from Career 1.0 to Career 3.0—you are the reason I consider myself lucky.

Scan QR code to access the
Penguin Random House India website